## Praise for *Round We*

"This book is a wealth of resources for creating a meaningful spiritual p without dogma and without a prescribed set of beliefs and structures. From a foundation of science and critical thinking combined with creativity, Mark A. Green has provided support for creating practices and rituals that reconnect us to the natural world, to each other, and to our inner wisdom. This is real magic—rekindling the awe and wonder of being alive."
—**SELENE KUMIN VEGA, PHD,** psychotherapist and Saybrook University professor

"I felt a bit overwhelmed trying to decide how I want to celebrate holidays and what I want to do as a personal practice. Not only have I really enjoyed implementing some of the suggestions in this book, but reading it also sparked some of my own ideas that are now scribbled in the margins. I highly recommend this book to anyone interested in learning some new ways to celebrate the phases of the year or about ritual in general. I feel filled with energy to go out and celebrate this amazing place we call home and how I experience it."
—**REBECCA NORDHAUSER, MS,** software engineer and an Atheopagan Society Council member

"Mark A. Green takes us by the hand and leads us on a journey. Along the way we learn to create science-based practices for improving our well-being, living in greater harmony with nature, and building a connected, authentic life. Accessible, well-organized, and useful, this book is both a road map and a companion, encouraging us to make the path our own."
—**RACHEL BEAL,** licensed counselor

"This book is a fundamental primer for building a solid practice in ritual. It brings what seems to be pure magic down to earth, allowing everyone to crack open the many aspects of a ritual life. It gives us the opportunity to include others with common values through ritual. All the little details are explained so there can be a good understanding of building rituals and activities for different occasions. I want to hug the book and keep it close."
—**DRIS BOBILIN,** fine artist and photographer

# Round We Dance

## About the Author

A thirty-five-year veteran of the United States' Pagan community, Mark Green is a poet, a singer, a ritualist, a nonprofit executive, and an activist. He founded the largest environmental organization in his region, Sonoma County Conservation Action, and was recognized by Congress and the California State Legislature for this work.

Mark is active in the Atheopagan community and serves as a Councilmember of the nonprofit Atheopagan Society. He has presented workshops and lectures on non-theist Paganism at such conferences as Pantheacon and The Conference on Current Pagan Studies, and to atheist and Unitarian Universalist groups all over the United States. This is his third book.

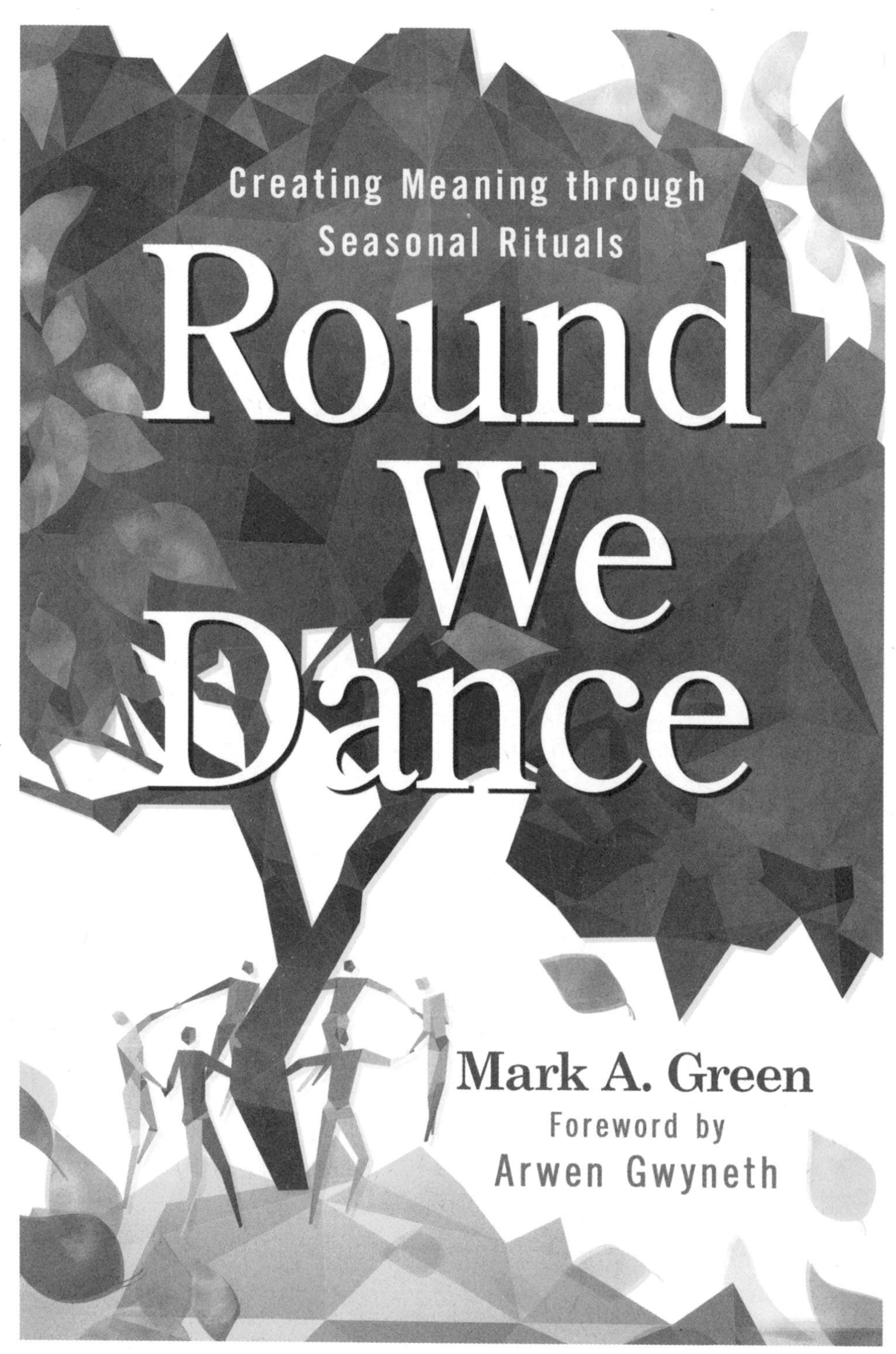


Llewellyn Publications
Woodbury, Minnesota

First Edition
First Printing, 2024

Cover design by Shannon McKuhen
Editing by Marjorie Otto
Interior art by
Corn Dolly and Wheel of the Year by the Llewellyn Art Department
Suntree Logo by the Atheopagan community



**Library of Congress Cataloging-in-Publication Data (Pending)**
ISBN: 978-0-7387-7536-4



Llewellyn Publications
A Division of Llewellyn Worldwide Ltd.
2143 Wooddale Drive
Woodbury, MN 55125-2989
www.llewellyn.com

Printed in the United States of America

# Dedication

This book is dedicated to the Atheopagan community, and particularly to those who have been Patreon supporters of my work or have volunteered as moderators, event organizers or members of the Atheopagan Society Council. Whether we interact on social media, video conferencing or in person, I have found you interesting, creative, thoughtful, generous, heart-felt and filled with kindness, and I cannot say enough about how knowing you has enhanced my life. Sharing rituals and fellowship with you is one of my life's great pleasures.

My love and thanks to you all.

## Acknowledgments

This book could not have come about if not for the support of my beloved partner Nemea, the incredible generosity in every sense of the Dark Sun ritual circle (Lisa Beytia, John Buffalo Brownson, Candace Hammond, Deborah Hamouris, DunKane Leonard, Selene and Rene Vega, Robin Weber), Colette Wendt and Joe Veahman, the wonderful gang of the Saturday Atheopagan Zoom Mixers, the Live Oak Circle (the Northern California Atheopagan affinity group), all members past and present of the Atheopagan Society Council (and particularly Arwen Gwyneth, my co-host on THE WONDER: Science-Based Paganism podcast), my generous Patreon supporters, the good folks of the Fire Circle Family and the Spark Collective, members of the Unitarian Universalist Congregation of Santa Rosa's Covenant of Unitarian Universalist Pagans (CUUPs) group, all the thousands of people I have circled with in ritual and discussed Paganism and ritual with over the past thirty-five years, and Kiki the Circus Cat, who keeps me delighted on a daily basis.

I'd also like to shout out to the staff and patrons of The Final Edition, a neighborhood, working-class kind of place that put up with the weird guy pounding away on the laptop for months, while I ordered non-alcoholic beer and didn't interact with anyone but the bartender.

# Contents

Foreword by Arwen Gwyneth (Yucca) xi

Introduction 1

## Part 1: A Primer

**Chapter 1:** Spirituality 9

**Chapter 2:** About Rituals 21

**Chapter 3:** Ritual Basics 27

**Chapter 4:** A Practice for Yourself 49

**Chapter 5:** Ritual Skills 55

**Chapter 6:** Ritual Arts 67

## Part 2: Rituals in Practice

**Chapter 7:** Occasions for Celebrating Rituals 91

**Chapter 8:** Rites of Passage 113

**Chapter 9:** Working with the Dead and Dying 129

**Chapter 10:** Personal and Healing Rituals 139

**Chapter 11:** Building Community for Sharing Rituals 153

**Chapter 12:** Beyond Rituals: Living the Spiritual Life 159

**Conclusion:** Welcome to the Journey! 173

## Part 3: Resources

Seasonal Crafts 177

Seasonal Recipes 199

Guided Meditations 213

Recommended Ritual Music 225

Glossary 229

Annotated Further Reading and Online Resources 235

Works Cited 239

# Foreword

by Arwen Gwyneth (Yucca)

In one of my earliest memories, I was a small child curled up in a sleeping bag on my father's lap.

Each evening he would quietly sit outside alone. That night, I finally got to join him.

A moonless sky stretched from horizon to horizon above us. Splashed across it were so many stars there hardly seemed room to fit more in the spaces between each sparkling point. The Milky Way was like a textured river of dozens of shades of black and purple.

Held in those safe arms, gazing silently into the depths of sky, I had for the first time that sense, now so familiar and welcome, of utter awe at the immensity of the Universe. Awe at the sheer number stars, and vastness of the night. I felt amazement that I was part of it, and yet so, very, very *tiny*.

Somewhere along the way, I had gotten it in my child's mind that stars were the "seeds" of life, scattered across the heavens like dandelion in the wind.

In the years to come, that idea would grow into the knowledge of elements, and stellar lifecycles, resource cycling, and ecosystem functions. It would grow into a love of the songs crickets chirped before dawn, and a curiosity for why the wind always seemed to blow from the southeast in the summers. It grew into desire for knowledge.

Many more nights under the stars, and mornings watching as our planet turned to face the Sun, led to a profound gratitude and the sometimes uncomfortable understanding that my time—our time—as conscious bits of this vast, magnificent world, is only a fleeting moment, barely even a blink of the eye.

Experiences like these have led myself and many others to seek ways we can live our short lives in fully present, eyes open, and joyful ways. We seek and cultivate tools and practices to help us not only better understand the world and ourselves, but also help us navigate and direct our lives as human creatures. Ways that embrace the poetry and richness of the night sky, of waves crashing against the shore, but are also grounded in scientific understanding.

Nature is spectacular in its own right. There is no need for the supernatural. We don't need gods, or fairies, or magical beings to understand the world. Nor do we need them to tell us how to live. We are fully capable of evaluating, deciding, and acting on what we believe is right or appropriate.

Many of us strive for ways to live that value truth, honor life and beauty, and seek to nurture love.

In 2016, I was fortunate to encounter Mark Green in the comments section of a YouTube video I had published titled "No, You Don't Have to Believe in Gods to be Pagan."

Pagan is an umbrella term that encompasses many difference religious practices, beliefs, and traditions. Some joke that the only thing all Pagans have in common is that they all call themselves pagan. This certainly reflects my experience! There are many, many different ways to be Pagan.

Some (very vocal) forms of Paganism embrace the belief in supernatural, deities, and magic as literal truths. But within Paganism there is another branch which takes a naturalistic approach. Off the branch of naturalistic

Paganism, there are various different traditions which seek non-supernatural but spiritual ways to be in the world. One of these is Atheopaganism.

In the comments of my nontheist pagan YouTube video, Mark invited me to check out the Atheopagan Facebook group. And I am glad I did!

The group was a wonderful breath of fresh air. It was full of hundreds of other like-minded, truth-seeking, ritual-practicing Pagans. They were kind, and enthusiastic. We could share photos of our Focuses (altars), holiday decorations, pets and nature walks, or discuss meditation techniques and the latest research on neuroplasticity.

One discussion that would come up time and time again was what resources were available for those of us interested in the richness of ritual, myth, and other "Pagan-y" things, without the superstitious and theist elements? There was a clear need for something like a podcast.

Mark and I began to chat and discuss the possibility of teaming up.

We launched THE WONDER: Science-Based Paganism podcast in early 2020, just weeks before COVID-19 lockdowns began.

Almost every single Saturday since then, Mark and I have met over Zoom to discuss everything from how we celebrate the Wheel of the Year, how to set up and use a Focus, ritual techniques, thoughts on gratitude, dealing with one's inner critic, to current events in the Pagan community.

We have been blown away by the thoughtful responses and encouragement from listeners.

I am grateful for what the podcast has become in the Atheopagan community, the role that it has played, and am deeply grateful for my friendship with Mark that has grown from it.

The podcast has become a highlight of my week. Each episode is an opportunity to reflect on how to live in a more joyful, present, and intentional way. It provides a means to give back to a growing community.

Humans are social animals. While there are times that solitude can nourish us, we can also be fed by the support and love of those around us, both physical and online. A sense of belonging is critical for our health and happiness.

One of the most exciting things to emerge over the past few years is recent growth in the Atheopagan community. Each new live gathering, ritual, social media comment, blog post, podcast episode, and now new book chapter is like another star in that beautiful twinkling night sky.

I look forward to seeing what constellations will come from this book.

# Introduction

Humans thrive when they feel meaning in their lives, joy in living, and connection in community.

Those are things that don't just happen. They have to be cultivated.

They have to be created.

Too often in our modern world, we fill our time with busyness, acquisition of money or possessions, or pursuit of fleeting pleasures. Those can provide a momentary sense of happiness, but they don't last: they are "empty calories" that soon wear off. Which is why alienation and loneliness are so often cited as top concerns in polls about mental health.

I've lived some of those struggles. I grew up in a hostile environment and have suffered chronic depression since grade school. Thankfully, it has been in remission for ten years, with good medication and practices.

This book is about finding more sustaining nourishment that brings deep contentedness with our lives: the celebration of moments, large and small, that help us to understand our lives as worthwhile and joyous, to feel connected with our fellow humans and creatures, to feel a worthy part of the magnificent Universe of which we are a part.

A powerful means to these ends is to have a spiritual practice. Maybe that involves activities you perform daily, if that's what you like, or maybe just a handful of times every year. But having them—practices and rituals that bring you into that sense of meaning and connectedness—can mean all the difference between a rather hollow life and one overflowing with moments of joy.

For many of us, having a spiritual practice and creating rituals is something completely new, because we have never done it before. Particularly for those who are atheists, agnostics or religiously unaffiliated, it can feel awkward to start the practices and activities of spirituality. Rituals, particularly, can feel a bit silly to begin with.

When you first start doing rituals as a person who has never had a ritual practice, it can feel contrived and hokey and uncomfortable. While we go through the steps of the ritual, the critical voice that each of us bears within us is yammering "This is stupid, you're making a fool of yourself." The ritual can also feel good, but the discomfort of that internal voice can undermine the sense of rightness or meaning rituals can bring.

I know because I went through it. It's been thirty-five years now, but I remember only too well how uncomfortable I was at my first ritual, when first confronted with joining a group standing in a circle holding hands, calling out earnestly my wishes and hopes, drumming and dancing—all of it. Fortunately, the parts that seemed most embarrassing and challenging to participate in—the parts where participants talked to unseen, noncorporeal presences like gods and spirits—turned out to be the ones I found, years later, I could dispense with.

The challenge for many of us who move in the direction of ritual observances is that our culture lauds the analytical, "thinky" part of the brain, and many of us are accustomed to living there as much as they can. And that is the exact part of the brain you want largely to turn off during ritual, which is much more akin to dancing, making music, creative playing or making art: "feely" stuff.

Where I'm going with this, skeptics and uncomfortable friends, is to encourage you to *keep going*. Being able to relax and submerge into the ritual state and tame that nattering, negative internal voice is a learned skill.

It gets easier. And the rewards are tremendous.

So—who am I to say so, and to write this book?

I'm Mark—by profession a nonprofit executive and fundraising professional, by vocation a seeker, poet, nature lover, science geek, costuming nerd, and tabletop roleplaying gamer.

As I write this, I have been steadily working for more than thirty years to bring my life and worldview into more alignment with verifiable reality, with living meaningfully and with joy.

This is not a simple problem. Many, for example, opt for worldviews that defy what science tells us about the Universe because they so intensely want for their gods or spirits or angels or what have you to be real. Many who reject religion, on the other hand, settle into nihilism and cynicism, with a bitter view that life is inherently and inextricably meaningless.

As the book unfolds, I will tell a bit of the story of my journey to where I am today in relation to these questions, but for now, suffice it to say that I have done a lot of this work for you. If you, like me, are searching for more meaning and joy in life and a sense of being connected to the Universe and in community, this book could be just what you are looking for.

## Atheopaganism

This book is intended to be used by anyone to enhance their happiness and sense of meaning in life through introduction of ritual practices enacted at meaningful moments. If that is why you got it, great!

However, the contents here emerge from a particular science-based spiritual path, *Atheopaganism*, so the following section contains a concise explanation of this path, its origin, and its values. In Atheopaganism, practitioners develop their own practices of rituals and celebrations within a seasonal framework and embrace a common-sense set of ethical precepts known as the 13 Atheopagan Principles. No belief in the supernatural (including gods of any kind) is involved.

Atheopaganism is a modern approach to spirituality based in solid science and intended to enhance the happiness, mental health, and effectiveness of its practitioners without claims of magic, gods, souls, afterlives, or other unverified phenomena.

I like to say it is a spirituality of the verifiably real.

Those who are interested in learning more about Atheopaganism should consider reading my previous book, *Atheopaganism: An Earth-Honoring Path Rooted in Science.* It goes into details about how religion engages the various systems of the human brain and how we can leverage these effects to benefit us. But for the purposes of this work, a brief overview will set the context for a guide to creating rituals which will help us to be happier, better, and more effective people.

A great many of the moments of joy and meaning in my life are times I have spent with loved ones, ritually celebrating the turning of the seasons and the changes in our lives. I have those events, those golden moments, because I cultivate them: because I have a spiritual practice.

This does not mean I subscribe to woo-woo beliefs about invisible beings and magical forces, about omens and portents. No.

I don't believe any of that stuff.

It means I have elected to pay attention to what is going on around me and celebrate. I choose to note the changes in the light as summer fades to autumn, and the first wildflowers in spring. I take time for sunsets and moonrises. I smell flowers and savor delicious meals.

I create memorable moments of emotional intensity and joy by designing and implementing rituals, both solitarily and with others.

This book will lay out principles and practices and ritual outlines so that you, too, can cultivate a life gaudily adorned with moments of joy, beauty, and happiness, either alone or shared with others.

The dominant culture around us is suspicious of pleasure—it equates enjoyment with "sin" and indulgence and encourages us to feel shame when enjoying perfectly normal things like food and sex and childlike play, or even when "feeling too much" in joy or grief or sadness. It encourages us to feel dirty and stained by some inherent flaw ("original sin") within us that we need redeemed. This is the ideology of the dominant religions in our society, and even those who don't subscribe to those beliefs are affected by them, having been raised immersed in a society that is suffused with them.

I reject absolutely the idea of the inherent wrongness of deep feeling, including enjoyment of pleasure. So long as no one nor the planet itself is being harmed by my enjoyment, I choose joy. I choose to eat my life with both hands, juice running down my chin. I intend to wring every moment of joy I can out of it, so that on my deathbed, if I am fortunate enough to have time to reflect, I will think, "What a wonderful adventure!"

This is why I wrote this book: to help others have an opportunity to find joy and fulfillment and meaning and celebration in their lives, as I do in mine.

Ritual practice can open a whole new dimension to life that is filled with meaning, kindness, joy, love, and emotional healing. It can make us wiser and better people.

So take a deep breath and begin. Do solitary rituals at first, so you don't have to feel self-conscious about being seen by others. Then, when ready, and if it seems appropriate to you, share your rituals with your family or friends.

And try to keep a straight face. It won't be too long before the thought of rolling your eyes never even occurs to you.

Enjoy the journey!

# Part 1
# A Primer

# Chapter 1
# Spirituality

You might well ask, what is spirituality? Why would I want to cultivate mine?

Spirituality is the human impulse to develop a sense of meaning and joy in life, connectedness with our fellow humans, and deeper purpose in living than simple survival. The spiritual impulse seeks answers to profound questions, like: who am I, really? What is the nature of the Universe? How should I live? What meaning can I find in living? What is Sacred—worthy of cherishing and safeguarding?

Many spiritually motivated people join established institutional religions or study philosophy in search of pre-packaged answers to such questions. Others, like me, choose to explore the nature of themselves and their world on their own.

What is a religion or spiritual path, exactly? Having studied and considered this question, I believe the answer is a simple three-part formula, which applies to any religion or spirituality that can be observed in the world:

**A Religion or Spiritual Path =**
**A COSMOLOGY + A SET OF VALUES + A SET OF PRACTICES**
**... all of which address human needs for meaning,**
**community and purpose in living.**

## Atheopaganism

Atheopaganism is a naturalistic religious path: that is to say, its worldview (or cosmology) assumes that all phenomena in the Universe are physical in nature and subject to physical laws. This is the consensus of what we have learned through scientific inquiry, and to date there is no credible evidence to the contrary. In other words, Atheopagans view the Universe the way modern, peer-reviewed science does: as an evolving set of physical processes, governed only by the laws of physics, and without supernatural phenomena such as god/desses, spirits, souls, or magic.

Atheopagans hold as Sacred the living Earth: the biosphere. It is what gave rise to humanity and, to this very minute, puts forth every breath in our lungs and morsel of food in our mouths. Earth-focused spiritual paths meet one definition of *Paganism,* which is a rapidly growing movement of alternative spirituality. Pagan paths typically draw inspiration from pre-Christian European religious traditions such as the Greek, Celtic, Norse, etc. Most modern Paganism (sometimes called Neopaganism) is a "re-imagining" of the values and practices of such earlier cultures, although most Atheopagans do not do so, being content to simply understand our path as a modern invention.

There's nothing wrong with that! In our modern world, we don't choose medieval medical practices, for instance, nor Bronze Age technology, and there is no reason why our spiritual practices should not also draw on all that humanity has learned up until the present. Just because ideas are old does not make them accurate or worthy.

As practitioners of Atheopaganism do not believe in gods, and are therefore *atheists,* and are also *Pagans*, I named this particular path "Atheopaganism" after developing the ideas and practices that it is comprised of.

There are other naturalistic religious or spiritual paths, such as naturalistic Judaism and Buddhism, and other varieties of naturalistic Paganism as well. Atheopaganism isn't the only way to have a naturalistic approach to spirituality.

You may agree with some, all, or none of the Atheopagan perspective. That's okay; this book's guidance will still be useful to you in building or enhancing ritual practices of your own that will enhance your experience of living.

Atheopaganism's values set forth four Sacred Pillars, which describe what is to be considered of value and worthy of care and stewardship (or *sacred)*, and thirteen ethical *Principles,* which are guidelines for how to live a happy life and be a good person.

The **Sacred Pillars** are our core beliefs about what is valuable, what is worthy of service and protection:

- **Life:** Meaning, the biosphere, the fabric of life on Earth. Not to be confused with individual lives (which die all the time—that's the way of things), this Pillar is our commitment to be respectful and grateful to the natural systems that enable and sustain life on Earth. Atheopagans are environmentalists.
- **Love:** Love is what connects us. It is what builds our families, bridges our disagreements, and heals our wounds. Atheopagans believe love (which necessarily implies mutual consent) in all its forms is sacred.
- **Truth:** What is true matters. When we make decisions based on falsehoods, harm results. Atheopagans apply critical thinking, the scientific method, and Occam's razor in our assessment of the nature of the world.
- **Beauty:** The aesthetic beauty of nature has a value unto itself. Nature's awe-inspiring complexity and magnificence is a source of inspiration and joy and well-being to Atheopagans. Note that this Pillar refers to the beauty of nature, not to human personal

appearance standards, which are often arbitrary and contribute to discrimination against those who do not meet them.

## The 13 Atheopagan Principles

Obviously, everyone has their own moral compass. We act according to what we view as right and proper; even when we are breaking our own supposed values, there is always a rationalization for why this action meets some higher good (even if it's just personal benefit). Atheopaganism isn't trying to supplant the internal moral landscape of its adherents, nor to establish arbitrary "commandments" that supply an external moral dictum, as do the Abrahamic religions. We are not a doctrinaire or dogmatic path.

What the Principles are intended to do is to spell out the moral landscape within which Atheopaganism makes sense. If the four Sacred things are truly held as Sacred, if Life is revered and Love is honored and Truth is pursued and Beauty is cherished, the result is a set of principles for living very much like the 13 Principles as articulated in this book.

Atheists are sometimes accused of having no morals, because the dominant culture is unable to conceive of morals and ethics that arise from the moral code and character of the individual, rather than as enforced by threat of punishment by a deity.

That accusation is baseless in fact. Everyone but a sociopath has their own sense of right and wrong and acts more or less in accordance with it. In the words of atheist and stage magician Penn Gillette, "I murder exactly as much as I want to. And that amount is zero." But it is a canard that persists in polling on public views on atheism, and one with which those of us who are nonbelievers must contend.

The Atheopagan Sacred Pillars and Principles are a way of spelling out what most who love the Earth believe anyway: that we must be kind, care for the Earth, be people of integrity, embrace diversity, and apply critical thinking in our assessments of what is likely to be true. They are meant to guide us along the way of our lives, to help us live as well and happily as we can, and to spread that happiness. These are the 13 Atheopagan Principles:

1. **Skepticism and Critical Thinking:** *I recognize that the metaphorical is not the literal.* Science and poetry are both of value, but they are not the same thing—we inquire skeptically to seek truth. This Principle encourages us to think rationally about propositions that are presented to us and to examine our own beliefs in light of the available evidence. It asks of us that we understand what constitutes a credible claim versus one that isn't very believable, and to recognize valid evidence from credible sources. If we apply critical thinking and a skeptical approach to our beliefs in the world, we are more likely to be acting based on what is actually true.
2. **Reverence:** *I honor the Earth, which produced and continues to sustain humanity.* Reverence doesn't mean submission or fawning obedience. It means to honor, to hold as worthy of the highest respect. Our planet certainly deserves this, as we are products of the fabric of Life through the process of evolution and continue to be sustained with every breath and mouthful of food by the Earth's systems. If we don't honor the Life-giver, what, then, should we?
3. **Gratitude:** *I am grateful for the gifts life presents me.* Gratitude is an essential life skill for happiness. It is so easy to focus on problems and complaints, but to live a life of contentment and occasional joy, we *must* note to ourselves those wonderful things that come to us, whether it's a particularly magnificent sunset, the scent of a rose on your morning walk, or something rare and amazing like a comet or the aurora borealis. Building a habit of gratitude helps us to grow, to deepen in happiness, and to spread that happiness around.
4. **Humility:** *I am humble, understanding that all humans are equal in deserving of dignity and respect.* Note that this is not inconsistent with having healthy self-esteem: rather, it is a warning against putting on airs and lording over others or believing ourselves to

be entitled to powers, considerations, or privileges that others are not. Note that one aspect of this Principle is the concept of *consent*. If we respect others as much as ourselves, we do not try to take advantage of them or presume that we can have their attention or touch them without their permission.

5. **Perspective and Humor:** *I laugh a lot… including at myself.* Atheopagans try to keep a "big picture" view and not take ourselves too seriously, understanding that "not sweating the small stuff" and keeping a good sense of humor is a way to improve our overall quality of life and to keep ourselves humble. This Principle isn't about mocking others or having humor at their expense; rather it is about incorporating humor and perspective to help reduce our stress and help us to get along better with others.
6. **Praxis:** *I enact regular ritual in observance of my celebration of life.* That's what this book is about! Here you can learn how to create effective rituals to improve the emotional depth and sense of celebration and meaning in your life.
7. **Inclusiveness:** *I celebrate diversity and am respectful of difference, be it of color, ethnicity, sex, gender, sexual orientation, ability, social class, or body shape.* No one on Earth is born superior. We are all worthy of respect, kindness, and consideration.
8. **Legacy:** *I recognize and embrace my responsibility to the young and future generations.* Atheopagans understand that we have an inherent responsibility to seek to leave a healthy and kind world to coming generations of humanity.
9. **Social Responsibility:** *I acknowledge that freedom is tempered by responsibility, and I have responsibility to others.* Humans are social animals, and we have responsibilities to each other, not only to ourselves and our immediate families. In our conduct, our activism, and how we vote, Atheopagans are considerate

of our impacts on others, particularly those less fortunate than ourselves.

10. **Pleasure Positivity:** *I celebrate pleasure as inherently good, so long as others are not harmed in its pursuit and the Four Pillars are respected.* This Principle is a direct rejection of the Calvinistic shame-cultivating, joy-phobic culture that dominates much of the world. It can be a real struggle to cleanse ourselves of that shame and truly to embrace enjoyment, but it is a liberating struggle we can all benefit from. Let us enjoy life!
11. **Curiosity:** *I understand that knowledge is never complete.* There is always more to be learned, and this means we need to keep our minds open to new information that may change our opinions or ways of seeing the world. Besides, curiosity means we are *interested* in the goings-on of the world, and being interested is a way to stay engaged and to keep your mind lively.
12. **Integrity:** *I conduct myself with fair dealing in word and deed.* This one is pretty clear. Being someone who stands by their word and is honest in their dealings contributes directly to having a happier and less complicated life.
13. **Kindness and Compassion:** *I practice kindness and compassion with others and myself.* This includes recognizing that they and I will not always meet the standards set by these principles.

In the end, having a generous inclination toward others, seeking to understand things from their viewpoint and acting toward them as they hope to be treated is its own reward: you will be received with greater kindness and compassion in turn. This final Atheopagan Principle is an encompassing guideline: *just be kind.* Even if it seems really hard to do in a given circumstance, it's usually the best course.

---

All of this said, using this book doesn't suggest that you "have to" do anything. These ideas are available to you as guidance and an opportunity to incorporate practices and observances into your life that will add richness, color, and joy. Adapt them as you see fit, holding in mind that the path was created with the intention of holding sacred those four Sacred Pillars.

For myself, I find that the Atheopagan Principles help to remind me of who I want to be when I feel uncentered or angry. They remind me who I am when I am my best self. I don't always live up to them. But I'm glad that they're there, and that the 13th Principle spells out that while no one will meet all those qualities all the time, we must be compassionate with ourselves and others when we don't.

I hope that you find value in them, too. But if not, all anyone can ask is that you be a person of kindness and integrity by your own lights. Because it's not about asserting "rules." It's about cultivating ways of living that increase happiness, both in yourself and those around you. You will find that if you do choose to live according to Atheopagan Principles, your life will become easier, kinder, less abrasive.

I sometimes describe Atheopaganism as religion with agency. In other words, instead of having a submissive, supplicating relationship with the Sacred, asking it for rules to follow and fearing punishment if we don't, we are empowered as Atheopagans to explore, discover, evolve, and celebrate our lives and our world as our own moral compasses and minds lead us to do.

## How Did Atheopaganism Come About?

In 1987, a friend invited me to an autumnal equinox ritual with his Pagan group. Pagans, as I understood it, were people who felt a deep connection with nature, and celebrated this with symbolic rituals that brought them happiness.

I had been a rational, naturalistic believer in science, critical thinking, and reason for all my life. But I went. To this day, I don't entirely know why.

The ritual was a little awkward for me. There was drumming and dancing. The standing-in-a-circle-holding-hands part was a bit uncomfortable to a buttoned-down, stiff guy like me. The "priestess" called out to invisible presences, though that seemed much more like a symbolic action than that people actually believed they existed.

But on the other hand... it was the autumnal equinox. That's a real thing, a real event in the natural world: the day in September when the lengths of the day and the night are equal (at the equator).

When was the last time I had noticed the solstices and equinoxes? How connected was I, a committed environmentalist, to the reality of what is happening on Planet Earth?

There was a lot to like about the Paganism I first encountered. My co-celebrants' joy in the turning of the seasons and the natural world appealed to my love for nature, and lent meaning to the passing of time. The people were warm and friendly, bright and creative, interesting and... free, somehow.

So I went to another gathering. I began to befriend the community of people who held them. The rituals began to feel natural, and I began to see glimpses of a wildness and freedom and gratitude and love for the Earth that were refreshingly different from the dominant culture with its shame and greed and emptiness.

That resonated with me. It suddenly made sense to me: that this is a way we should live, aware of the rhythms of the Earth, honoring it and grateful for all it provides for us.

I became a Pagan, and, with time, a leader in my local Pagan community.

This went on for nearly twenty years.

Yes, people in most of the rituals were "invoking gods" and talking to invisible qualities like "the spirits of air, fire, water, and earth." But, I reasoned, they were pretending, right? Surely they understood that these ancient gods and goddesses were imaginary myths?

This is what I told myself. For all that time, I was a happy Pagan atheist. In those days we didn't discuss our personal beliefs much; we just held our rituals and celebrated being in a creative, joyous community together.

Then, around the year 2000, things began to change.

For one thing, some people in the community—mostly newcomers, former Christians—started talking about the importance of believing in gods; about how you "couldn't really be a Pagan" if you didn't.

After a few years of increasingly loud adjurations in community communications that only believing in gods in a literal sense made someone a "real Pagan," I had a series of deeply disturbing experiences that soured me on the community and made me realize just how literally many within it were taking this deity stuff.

I quit going to Pagan events, let my altar gather dust. I was through. I wasn't going to be a part of something so divorced from reality and willing to excuse unethical behavior.

But something strange happened about six months later: I was unhappy. I felt disconnected from the world, disconnected from myself. My sense of place in the Universe and joy in living had dissipated. I missed the feeling of my Pagan practice.

I started mulling some questions and doing some research, and then I wrote an essay about what I proposed to practice—a sort of manifesto, to organize my thinking and establish the rational basis for the practice I began to implement, which I was now calling *Atheopaganism*.

I cleaned and began working again at my altar, which I began to call a *Focus* as a confirmation to myself that that is what it is for: not worship, not sacrifice.

The joy and meaning I had been missing returned, even more strongly.

Then, something amazing happened. Friends to whom I had shown my essay said that it was interesting, and I should post it online. So I did.

Suddenly, people both online and at Pagan events started confiding to me, "I read your essay. That's what I believe, too!"

I created a Facebook group. People started joining the group: first in dozens, then in hundreds, then thousands. I launched a blog at *Atheopaganism.org,* where I published support guides for creating rituals and living the path I had laid out. The Facebook community developed a logo for Atheopaganism: the *Suntree.* It looks like this:

***Suntree logo***

I discovered that there were others who were practicing nontheist, science-consistent Paganism, too, under names like *humanistic Paganism* or *naturalistic Paganism* or *secular witchcraft*. I connected with them, learned from them, widened the circle.

Over and over, as newcomers arrived in this newly-formed Atheopagan online community, I read statements like these:

"I'm an atheist, and my life has been feeling like it's missing something. This intrigues me, and I'm going to give it a try."

"I'm surrounded by literal theists in my coven. I'm a scientist, and I just can't. Thank you for articulating what I believe and do."

"I feel like I have come home."

It's been heartwarming and confirming to hear these testimonials. What we are building as a community is something that is meeting deep human needs for many people in the world now, and I could not be more humbled or gratified.

Since, I have devoted myself to publishing ideas and thoughts for Atheopagans and those investigating the path, to help them develop their practices. My first book, *Atheopaganism: An Earth-Honoring Path Rooted in Science,* came out in 2019.

In 2020, we organized a nonprofit tax-exempt religious organization, the Atheopagan Society, to serve as a repository for the resources I had created and to provide support, produce events, and conduct training and education for Atheopagans.

## Your Path Is Yours

Just having picked up this book, you have everything you need to start your own practice. You can practice alone (as a "solitary") or connect with others of like mind to share your seasonal observances and rites of passage.

Now, there are other naturalistic religious paths. You don't have to elect to be an Atheopagan in order to gain benefit from the information and practices in this book. But it does offer one science-grounded, ethically kind, and deeply enjoyable and meaningful way to live a spiritual life. You always have choices, so think about each section after you read it: how does this sound to me? Does this make sense for my life?

Your life is yours. Only you can make a decision to opt into a path like Atheopaganism or something like it.

Let's dive in! Let's talk about rituals.

# Chapter 2
# About Rituals

Nearly everyone participates in rituals. Even those of us with no religious background attend weddings, funerals, birthday gatherings, graduation ceremonies and so forth. Most of us celebrate secularized holidays such as Christmas, Easter, and the American and Canadian Thanksgiving in some fashion, too. Each of these incorporates traditional rituals as well.

Rituals are *symbolic activities carried out in an intentional manner to evoke feeling or meaning in the celebrant or celebrants.* Purposes of rituals for someone who isn't a *theist* (a believer in one or more gods) may be to celebrate a particular season or holiday and its meanings, to observe a life passage such as a birth, wedding, or death, or simply to offer awe, gratitude, and reverence for the gifts of Life, of which we are all a part: to the Universe itself.

Now, there are other definitions of the word *ritual.* Some use it to mean "any action done habitually." For purposes of this book, however, such routine activities as making coffee in the morning or tying your shoes, though they are frequently repeated, aren't rituals. They're just habits.

Celebrating a ritual makes a moment that might otherwise seem ordinary into an occasion: an event to be savored and remembered. Rituals enrich a life and help to bring a sense of meaning to the passage of time. Rituals can reinforce devotion to values, bring renewed confidence in goals and interpersonal commitments, help us to grow and deepen self-esteem and self-respect, and help us to build community with like-minded people.

Humans have been practicing rituals since long before even the invention of agriculture.[1] Evidence of rituals involving offerings of stone tools to a python figure and dating to over 70,000 years old has been found in the Tsodilo hills of Botswana.[2] That's more than *ten times* older than agriculture, and twice as old as the oldest European Paleolithic cave paintings!

Today, people throughout the world practice rituals, big and small, whether they are elaborate royal coronations, an athlete's wearing a "lucky" jersey or having a special lucky way of knotting their shoes, or a simple beach wedding.

Scientific research has verified the psychological impact of human ritual.[3] We understand to some degree why rituals work, and why they are important to us. Depending on the culture, we celebrate rituals to acknowledge our religious and cultural traditions, the turning of the seasons, personal and familial milestones in life, and to focus our attention, our intention, and our future activity in pursuit of our goals.

It's important and meaningful stuff.

It bears saying, though, that the effects of rituals are psychological in nature. Ritual transforms the consciousness of the ritual's participants. It changes our focus, our mood, and our confidence. Ritual can rewrite inter-

1. Bachenheimer, Avi. *Gobleki Tepe: An Introduction to the World's Oldest Temple* (Birdwood), 2018.
2. The Research Council of Norway. "World's Oldest Ritual Discovered -- Worshipped The Python 70,000 Years Ago." ScienceDaily. ScienceDaily, 30 November 2006.
3. Anastasi, M.W. & Newberg, A.B. A preliminary study of the acute effects of religious ritual on anxiety. *Journal of Alternative and Complementary Medicine* 14, 163–165 (2008); Brooks, A.W., *et al.* Don't stop believing: Rituals improve performance by decreasing anxiety. *Organizational Behavior and Human Decision Processes* 137, 71–85 (2016); Norton, M.I. & Gino, F. Rituals alleviate grieving for loved ones, lovers, and lotteries. *Journal of Experimental Psychology: General* 143, 266–272 (2014); Foster, D.J., Weigand, D.A., and Baines, D. The effect of removing superstitious behavior and introducing a pre-performance routine on basketball free-throw performance. *Journal of Applied Sport Psychology* 18, 167–171 (2006).

nal narratives and heal psychological wounds. It is powerful and effective in doing these things.

Adding supportive rituals to our lives can enhance our self-esteem, beef up our confidence when we're under pressure, improve our focus and concentration for demanding tasks, and help us to deepen relationships with those around us.

However, though their effects upon us can be profound, there is no persuasive evidence that rituals can cause "magical" effects in the world, like influencing the behavior of other people or changing the weather. As naturalistic thinkers, our adherence to reason and critical thinking make it important to recognize this. If you want to change something in your life, a ritual can help you to be confident and focused in pursuing it, but you still need to take the physical actions to make it happen. It will not happen magically just because you did a ritual.

Rituals can help us to be happier! Turning what could be pedestrian events into celebrations adds to our enjoyment of life and our connection with others, which science tells us is good for us in many ways.

## How Rituals Work: The Science

Much of the ritual technique and technology shared in this book is designed with the intention of provoking a very particular state of mind in a ritual's participants: the *ritual state,* also sometimes called *trance,* or *flow.*

This is a brain state that hasn't been scientifically studied very much, despite the fact that people have been deliberately provoking the ritual state in themselves and their fellows for thousands of years. Formal study of the ritual state only began in the 1970s. But what researchers say about it is that it is the state of what athletes call "being in the zone": experiencing the present moment vividly, with extreme focus, competency, and confidence, and, often, with a rich overlay of personal meaning. Psychologists Jeanne Nakamura and Mihaly Csikszentmihalyi define this state as "optimal performance" with "complete absorption in what one does."[4] Unsurprisingly, it is

4. Csikszentmihalyi, Mihaly: *Flow: The Psychology of Optimal Experience* (Harper Perennial Modern Classics), 2008.

in this state that artists, athletes, and other peak performers do their best work.

Most of the ritual technologies we are familiar with are directly associated with provoking the ritual state. Repetitive rhythms as in drumming or electronic dance music; low, colorful and/or intermittently flickering light conditions such as by firelight or candlelight or light through stained glass; close harmonic chanting or singing, hypnotic speaking or reading of poetry; dreamy incense scents are all classic trance-inducing approaches that have been perfected by such traditions as the Roman Catholic and Eastern Orthodox churches … and dance clubs everywhere.

The ritual state feels good. It feels like both a surrendering of self-consciousness and a welling-up of possibility, focus, and power. It's no surprise that people have pursued it throughout human history.

But it is also a state in which psychological transformation can take place. By entering an emotionally vulnerable, open state, we can access our past injuries and our core beliefs, and by undergoing symbolic transformation activities, we can actually change these aspects of ourselves. We can recover from trauma; we can rewrite the stories of what has embittered or hurt us. Thus the section of this book on rituals of healing.

In fact, some who practice rituals for peak performance consider it "brain hacking": accessing the subconscious to optimize experience and performance.

A part of understanding the value of learning ritual skills is coming to know that these are techniques which can enable us to optimize our focus at will. A useful psychological tool kit for anyone, but particularly for those pursuing a path of personal growth and change. While in this state, psychological healing can take place, traumatic memories can be revisited and literally re-written, and cathartic, personally transformational states of ecstasy can be achieved. I have seen profound changes in people after going through a transformational ritual experience.

How do rituals affect us in this way? It all goes back to the well-publicized placebo effect, as well as involving some quirks about the way the human brain works.

The placebo effect is a well-documented phenomenon in medical research, which is the tendency of any medication or treatment, even an inert or ineffective one, to exhibit results simply because the recipient believes that it will work.[5]

In other words, patients who receive a "null" or "control" treatment without any actual medicine in it still demonstrate an improvement of symptoms relative to those who have not received any treatment at all. This is testimony to the power of our minds to affect our bodies and reveals a deep truth about what it means to be human: our beliefs can profoundly influence our experience, even of symptoms like pain, allergic reactions and so forth.

One fascinating thing about the placebo effect is that placebos can be effective in reducing symptoms *even when the patient knows they have been given a placebo.* It won't work as well as a "secret" placebo (and certainly not as well as actual medicine), but just taking a sugar pill—even when you know it is a sugar pill—will still have an effect on your symptoms in many cases.

This phenomenon is known as the "open label" placebo effect, and it is why acting as if magic works can be powerfully effective in transforming our feelings, perspectives, and beliefs. While at one level we are skeptical and know that a"magic knot" for a runner's shoes can't really change their athletic ability, at another the confidence of a person rises when they perform such rituals, and we all know that elevated confidence can lead to superlative performance.

We in the naturalistic religious world, including Atheopagans, practice what some practitioners call "spicy psychology" with ourselves: rituals that help us to enter the ritual state and encourage us to be motivated to achieve what we hope to, to focus, be confident, heal from our psychological wounds, and be the people of our highest aspirations.

5. Kelley, J. M., Kaptchuk, T. J., Cusin, C., Lipkin, S. & Fava, M. Open-label placebo for major depressive disorder: a pilot randomized controlled trial. *Psychother. Psychosom.* 81, 312–314 (2012); Schaefer, M., Harke, R. & Denke, C. Open-label placebos improve symptoms in allergic rhinitis: a randomized controlled trial. *Psychother. Psychosom.* 85, 373–374 (2016).

People do rituals to mark moments of gratitude and joy, solemn and meaningful occasions, even loss, rage, and grief. We use them to recognize important milestones in our lives. And we do them to work with our own psychologies, to focus our intentions, to heal our wounds, to express our relationships with our communities, and to find wisdom within ourselves.

The next section will walk you through the processes of creating rituals. With practice, you'll find they add an entirely new dimension to your experience of living.

# Chapter 3
# Ritual Basics

Ritual design is a creative art form. It can be really fun. Every individual has unique creative ideas that inform their rituals. There are as many ways to structure and conduct a ritual as there are people in the world.

But that said, we can take a step-by-step approach to ritual design that will help you create an effective ritual that is tailored exactly to what is meaningful and transformative to *you*. While it can be great to draw inspiration from rituals others have created, at the very least they usually need some adjustment to be exactly right for any given individual.

The steps presented here will walk you through planning and implementing an effective and meaningful ritual for yourself or for a group. You will need a few sheets of paper to create your plan. Enjoy this creative process of discovery!

1. **What is the purpose of your ritual?** Is it a seasonal or full Moon celebration, or a ritual to heal some inner hurt? A rite of passage of some kind, like a celebration of a birth or a wedding? A ritual for guidance and wisdom, or to align yourself with an intended purpose, or to get some perspective on a problematic situation? (For more information on occasions for rituals,

see chapter 7). Write out the purpose of your ritual as a short sentence.

2. **What are the emotional themes of your ritual?** Love? Anger? Fear? Sadness? Hope? Determination? A longing for freedom? Write out thematic elements of your ritual as words or short phrases.
3. **What's the atmosphere you would like to create in the ritual?** Is it hushed and fervent, or happy and upbeat, or wild and ecstatic, or spooky and witchy, or silly, or solemn and grave? Jot down adjectives that describe how you would like the ritual to feel.
4. **What symbols are meaningful to you in relation to that theme and atmosphere?** What things, tools, processes, or metaphors do you associate with your theme and atmosphere? Examples could include drawn symbols, flags, objects from nature, pictures of people or places, and objects that remind you of the theme (so, for instance, if you're working up a ritual to write in your journal more, you might include your favorite pen). List these symbols and objects.
5. **What sensory experiences do you associate with your theme?** Sight, sound, scent, taste, touch? List those. It's important to engage multiple senses so the brain can settle into the ritual state—a heightened state of presence and creativity also called "trance" and known by artists as flow. Is there music you associate with the theme, or sounds like the ocean or birdsong? The scent of flowers or a particular perfume or incense, or a particular color scheme? The flavor of lemonade, or red wine, or childhood candy? List those as well.
6. **What activities do you associate with themes and meanings of the ritual?** Is there a craft or art form that is germane to what you're creating your ritual for? Consider getting an example that suits your ritual theme. Do you have a memory of going to a

particular place that is associated with the theme? Use a picture of that place. List them, too.

---

All of the elements you have now captured are the raw materials for your ritual (you don't have to use all of them). Using our prior example of a ritual to increase the frequency of writing in your journal, you might have selected your favorite pen; your latest journal itself; a book that smells really good, like a library; and a candle as your objects. You may have identified the emotional tone you are hoping for as excited and motivated. Maybe "focused and centered" have been identified as the atmosphere you are hoping for in your ritual. You may have added a favorite coffee cup, because you associate it with writing time.

Now, take a break! Give your planning at least a couple of hours just to percolate in your mind. You may find yourself inspired by particular connections or images or imagining some kind of activity as a part of your ritual.

When you're ready, take your lists and descriptions and get a fresh sheet of paper. It's time to structure your ritual into an outline.

## Structuring Your Ritual: A Format

After planning your ritual, structure it using your source materials. On your fresh sheet of paper, create an outline for your ritual using the following technique. The structure shown here isn't required, and there are many other ways to structure rituals, but this one is tested and effective, and a good place to start.

The structure's six phases are Preparation, Arrival, Invocation of Qualities and Intentions, the Working (also known as "Deep Play"), Declarations of Gratitude, and Benediction. I will go through each phase separately.

### *Preparation*

The preparation phase involves creation of a space and emotional environment that are conducive to the psychological transformation intended by the ritual. This is also called *establishing sacred space.*

First and foremost, hold your ritual in a place where you are comfortable and are not going to be interrupted. This could be a living room or back yard, or it could be in a secluded part of a local park—whatever will best provide a sense of "magic" and security. It can be disastrous to a ritual and a real psychological blow to its participants to have an outsider barge into your circle in the middle of a ritual.

Create a safe, contained setting conducive to entering the ritual state by using lighting. (Firelight or candlelight are best—flickering and dim—but low light levels with Christmas lights or rope lights can also create a good light level. Think of the light levels provided by the stained glass windows in a Gothic cathedral, which is a masterful implementation of sacred space.) Overhead light is not advised. Remember, whenever working with open flame, it is essential to have a fire extinguisher or other means of putting out a fire should an accident occur.

Elements other than lighting that contribute to establishing sacred space include usage of scents such as incense, essential oils, or burning herbs; building Focuses (i.e., symbolic altars—see page 49) with visual cues that draw the eye and communicate meanings; and music, either performed by participants or recorded and played.

Don't forget to prepare yourself. Take a bath with a special scented soap or essential oils you only use for rituals. Eat lightly or even fast that day so it is easier to enter the ritual state. Dress in clothing that helps you to feel powerful and "magical": this might involve a full outfit such as a robe or special dress, and/or items of jewelry you only use in rituals. Sit in meditation on the ritual theme for a while before beginning the ritual. Be as present, ready, and primed for transformation as you can be; others will come along with you that much more easily.

While I prefer live drumming and percussion instrumentation in a group ritual, when I do solitary ritual, I often put on recorded ritual music. Some of my favorite albums include *Passion*, the soundtrack to *The Last Temptation of Christ* by Peter Gabriel; *In the Realm of a Dying Sun* and *The Serpent's Egg* by Dead Can Dance; *Offerings* by Vas; and *Stratosfear* by Tangerine Dream. See the resources at the end of the book for a more extensive list of recorded music conducive to effective rituals.

*The ritual begins when setup begins,* so be mindful as you place objects, light incense, etc. Be silent, speaking quietly only when necessary. Do your tasks with deliberation, focus and seriousness.

## *Arrival*

The goal of Arrival is induction of participants into the ritual state as described previously: a liminal "glowing" feeling of acute sensory awareness in the present moment, and typically of deep well-being. It is sometimes also referred to as trance or flow (or even, by people who are religious, as a "religious experience").

Challenges to be overcome by the Arrival phase for participants include preoccupation or thinking about the past or future; self-consciousness or cynicism, which is feeling embarrassed by or resistant to the prospect of entering the ritual state; and self-containment, or feeling separate from other participants, and uncomfortable with opening to them emotionally. The practices in the Arrival phase are designed to calm these effects and shift consciousness into preparedness for ritual work.

Arrival has several components, all or only some of which may be used in a given ritual. While not every ritual uses all of them, they are most effective when performed in the order shown. When ritual participants are used to working with one another, they may require fewer of these steps in order to enter the ritual state and be ready for transformative work.

### ENTERING THE NOW

Sudden stimulation of the senses can help celebrants to inhabit their senses and aid them in becoming present in the moment. Examples of techniques in this category are smoke blessings, including wafting or fanning scented smoke over each celebrant; burning herbs or incense; asperging (sprinkling) with water or scented water; use of a chime, singing bowl, rattle, didgeridoo or other instrument to outline the body in a sound blessing;

or administration of a sacramental taste of something flavorful—a single dark chocolate chip, for example, or a tiny sip of wine—to draw each participant's consciousness into the senses, into the present moment, into the sacred Now.

### CREATING CONNECTION

Creating connection is intended to reduce the sense of "social boundary" between celebrants. Example techniques can include having celebrants stand in a circle and hold hands, make eye contact with one another, and/or each speak their name. Connection (in group rituals) is important because it establishes a greater sense of safety and improves the ability of celebrants to surrender into the ritual state.

### GROUNDING

Grounding is the use of techniques such as guided meditations by spoken word to connect the celebrant with where she is in time and space, and to remind her of the vastness and beauty of the great Cosmos and of the living Earth. It is often helpful to coordinate this with awareness of breathing, as in mindfulness and meditation practices ("Take a deep breath through your nose; hold it for two seconds, then blow it out your mouth slowly for a five-count. Now another. Now a third, final time.") Grounding can be enhanced physically by such actions as standing with bare feet upon the Earth or holding a heavy stone. See later sections in the book for guidelines and more examples of guided meditations.

### EMBODIMENT

Embodiment is expansion of the felt sense of the ritual state to encompass the body. Techniques to achieve embodiment include a visualized "body scan" wherein participants focus on feeling each part of their bodies; musical activities such as toning or singing or a heartbeat drum (which results in swaying, slow movement); or upbeat drumming/music to provoke more active dancing. Bluesy/gospel-style chants and songs work well for embodiment—try to avoid staid Protestant-style hymnlike songs, as they are not very emotional and don't stimulate the ritual state. Continue singing/chanting until all participants are moving freely.

After these steps, participants will usually be in the ritual state and ready to do ritual work.

### *Invoking Qualities*

Qualities are attributes that participants would like to be with them and incorporated into the ritual as they conduct it. "Invoking Qualities" is often just that: A designated celebrant encourages the circle to call out the Qualities they would like to be a part of the ritual, and celebrants repeat them in response. Examples of Qualities invoked might include Compassion; Grief; Courage; Adventure; Strength; Health; Wisdom; Perseverance. It is more effective if, after each Quality is invoked, all participants repeat the word or phrase.

This can be done in "popcorn" fashion (randomly called out) or sequentially around the circle; it can be done singing, or even danced. There are probably hundreds of creative ways the Qualities can be invoked.

In some rituals there may be preassigned participants to invoke particular Qualities with more detailed invocations, similar to "calling the quarters" in a Wiccan/Neopagan ritual. In fact, special Focuses (see page 49) may be built on themes of these Qualities to evoke greater attention to them on the part of celebrants.

Note that if there is a particularly important Quality you want to be the central focus of your ritual, it should have a special invocation of its own. For example, if you are designing a ritual to help a job search, you might have special invocations for Confidence and Patience.

### *Declaring Intention (Optional)*

Many rituals have their intentions determined in advance, or their purposes are self-evident: to celebrate a holiday, for example. In these cases, declaring the intention of the ritual is not necessary, although celebrants may choose to do so. Some rituals do not have a clear and obvious intention, or may have multiple intentions. In the latter case, after the invocation of the Qualities, declaration of the intended effect of the ritual adds to the psychological power of the ritual and allows participants to add their own personal goals to the ritual's "mixture" if they so choose. A designated celebrant can declare the intention, or participants may be encouraged to call out their own.

### *The Working or "Deep Play"*

The Working or "Deep Play" is the main event of the ritual. It is the phase during which *transformation* occurs. In a more informal ritual, it can be free-form dancing—perhaps about a bonfire—with spontaneously offered chant, song, spoken word, drumming and music, or line or spiral dancing; it can be laying of hands on an ailing celebrant; it can be shared harmonic improvisational singing; it can be completing a craft project focused on a particular emotion, transformation or Quality while singing a chant; it can be the passing of a mirror from hand to hand as each celebrant contemplates their reflection to the sound of a heartbeat drum; it may be drumming and singing while each celebrant in turn makes an offering or performs an action. Literally anything that transforms consciousness and leads to change in accordance with the intention of the ritual can constitute the Working of a ritual.

Typically, that activity will:

#### STIMULATE

Either metabolically or contemplatively. Pulsing drumming (sometimes replaced by rhythmic recorded music), soaring harmonies, or calming/entrancing sounds like singing bells, tinkling chimes, the susurrus of a rain stick or a quiet flute melody can set the emotional tone for celebrants while they are conducting the ritual's Working/Deep Play activity.

#### COMMUNICATE MEANING

In the sense that what is done in the Working is freighted with metaphorical or symbolic meaning beyond the simple activity itself.

BRING EMOTIONAL CATHARSIS

In that the emotional journey of the ritual reaches its peak during the Working.

---

It is critically important that whatever activities take place in the circle during the Working must be tailored to aid celebrants in maintaining their ritual state—their condition of open, empowered Presence. Even in light-hearted ritual, there is an underlying seriousness to the work that must be honored. While stimulation is key, too much stimulation or the wrong emotional tone can "break the spell." Imagine the ritual state, the energy of a ritual as a soap bubble which must be kept aloft without breaking.

The potential palette of activities and emotional flavors of Deep Play is nearly infinite. This phase of ritual is where much of the opportunity for creativity and imagination in ritual design is found.

## *The "Energy Curve" of a Ritual*

Some Workings are designed to increase in felt emotional energy and build to an ecstatic climax; some to remain at a "steady boil" rather than to climb. Some may even rise and then fall to the point that at its end, there is only a fervent whisper of activity, and then silence. All are effective ways to work with the emotional feeling of Deep Play and may be selected for usage when appropriate.

Remember: transformation is the watchword. There will be a felt emotional shift in a successful ritual.

When the Working is completed—when all participants have completed its activity, the energy has climbed to a climax and then dwindled to a murmur—it is time to begin the dénouement of the ritual: Gratitude and Benediction.

## *Declarations of Gratitude*

When the Deep Play is done, it is time to express Gratitude. Gratitude is such a key element of a happy life that even when our rituals are to assuage fear or sorrow, we must always remember the many gifts with which we are showered by the Universe every day.

Gratitude is often declared in a manner similar to Invoking the Qualities, creating a kind of bookend effect: either going around the circle and having each celebrant express what they are grateful for, or doing so in random "popcorn" fashion. Celebrants may also express gratitude that the Qualities were with them in the circle, e.g., "I am thankful that Discipline is with me and supports the work I do here."

Gratitude is often combined with the sharing of ceremonial food and drink—a way for participants to feel their very bodies surging with gratitude as, say, a rich red wine or ripe strawberry or chocolate or freshly baked bread encounters their taste buds. *We are alive today*, says the phase of Gratitude, *Thank you for this, and for those who love us, and for all the great and small blessings we enjoy in this precious life we live.*

## *Benediction*

Benediction ("saying a good word") is the formal ending of the ritual: a declaration that the ritual is over, with an expression of well-wishing and encouragement that celebrants act in accordance with the intentions of the ritual as they move forward in their lives.

I prefer to end my rituals the same way most of the time, in the hope that my co-celebrants will learn this benediction and it will become something we can speak together, in unison.

My frequent benediction is this: "To enrich and honor the gift of our lives, to chart a kind and true way forward, by these words and deeds we name intent: *(participants join in unison)* to dare, to seek, to love. May all that must be done, be done in joy. We go forth to live!"

## *Example: A Ritual Outline*

Let's take, for instance, our example of a ritual to increase writing in a journal. Here is a sample outline a practitioner might create for such a ritual.

### PREPARATION

The practitioner has gone through the process previously described and selected the following elements for their ritual: a favorite pen; a journal; a book that smells really good; a candle; and a favorite coffee cup. They have identified the emotional tone hoped for as focused, excited, and motivated.

They take the tablecloth from the desk or table where they usually write and use it as the surface on which to lay out a Focus: the journal in the center, open, with the pen in the crease between the pages; the book off to one side of the journal, the coffee cup to the other, where it will be at hand. An unlit candle in a stand is directly above the journal, and a small dish containing burning charcoal is to the other side of the coffee cup.

### ARRIVAL

The practitioner puts on favorite music for writing and sits in their favorite writing chair before the Focus, eyes closed, breathing deeply until they feel a sense of presence and calm, of deliberation. They open their eyes and light the candle, seeing the warm glow wash over the journal and the other items. They sprinkle some powdered incense on the charcoal and smell the wafting, calming scent. They are ready.

### QUALITIES

Speaking calmly but firmly, the practitioner says aloud, "I call creativity, and focus, and inspiration, and diligence to help me in this work. I call the love of writing, the power of art, the joy of creation—be with me now!"

### WORKING

Continuing, the practitioner takes up the pen, uncaps it and writes on a fresh page in the journal, speaking the words as they write them: "I love writing in my journal. I learn about myself and capture the great moments of my life. My journal brings me happiness. I am ready to commit to write every other day at a minimum. I make this commitment in the name of bettering my life."

The practitioner sifts some more incense onto the charcoal so a fresh wave of scent rises into the air. Passing the pen through the smoke, they say, "I charge this pen with boundless creativity!" They cap the pen and place it along the top edge of the book.

GRATITUDE

"I am grateful for the extraordinary events of my life," they say. "For the many moments, great and small, that bring me joy and inspire me to write. I am even grateful for pain and sorrow when they help me to write in my journal. Thank you for my life and for the many gifts I receive as a part of this world."

BENEDICTION

Standing up from the table, the practitioner says, "I go forth as a *writer,* someone who writes regularly. I go forth with tools and powers, with inspiration and dedication. I go forth into a vivid life, one of learning and enjoyment. *I GO FORTH!*"

They blow out the candle. The ritual is over.

## Now You Do It!

Lay out a special Focus (a naturalistic word for an altar—see page 49) for your ritual to help create your mindset, using the symbols, tools, and objects you have identified as appropriate. Don't forget your sensory cues, like scents, music, and candles.

Prepare yourself; perhaps take a shower or bath, and/or don a special garment or jewelry.

Then begin.

If the outline for the ritual you have developed turns out not to be working or doesn't feel right, toss it! Improvise and go with what you feel.

Remember: in conducting a ritual, you seek to provoke the ritual state: a *feeling.* It is a state of heightened awareness and presence. There isn't a "wrong way" to do it. What works for you is the right way.

## Before and After a Ritual

Rituals can be physically taxing. They can work up your feelings and metabolic rate, and simply attaining and being in the ritual state of focus, presence, emotion, and awareness can burn a lot of energy.

Accordingly, we need to take care of our bodies and our minds prior to and following a ritual.

### *Prior to Preparation Phase*

Generally speaking, it is good to make oneself ready for a ritual by eating a light, healthy snack of some kind, like a piece of fruit, and ensuring that you are sufficiently hydrated. Get a good night of sleep the night before if at all possible.

There are exceptions to these rules. Sometimes fasting is employed in the lead-up to a ritual, or sleep deprivation, or both. These can contribute to a ritual being very emotionally impactful, but if these techniques are used they should be offset by a thorough grounding and return to a normal state after the ritual's closing.

Hydration is *always* a must. Unless the ritual is very short (say, thirty minutes) have water available for participants during a ritual and be sure you are sipping water, whether or not you feel you need it.

### *Post-Benediction Phase*

After a ritual, you may find yourself feeling light-headed or dreamy, still in the ritual state, or you may have had a profound emotional experience that is still lingering with you. The limbic system of the brain is highly activated during the ritual state; this creates an altered state of consciousness that can result in danger of clumsiness or lack of attentiveness when it comes to engaging with physical reality. Do not, for example, jump right in a car and drive while in this state.

Instead, do what you can to ground or reorient your body and mind to an ordinary state of consciousness. Eat something hearty: complex carbohydrates, fats, and proteins rather than sugars. Touch the soles of your feet or your bare palms flat against the Earth and just breathe for a few minutes, concentrating on your breath going in and out. Then sit quietly and just notice your surroundings: pay particular attention to their details. Soon, you will feel more normal and will be able to go about the business of cleaning up from the ritual and moving on with your day or night.

The ritual state is pleasurable and powerful, but it is also an altered state of consciousness and should not be combined with operating heavy machinery or other dangerous activities. Be sure to take care of yourself and those around you as you conduct your ritual work.

### *A Note on Using Psychoactive Substances in Ritual*

It is no secret that people have used various chemical substances—whether or not they happen to be legal where they are—to potentiate and intensify the ritual state of trance. Indigenous and Western practitioners alike have used alcohol, cannabis, psychedelic hallucinogens, and other substances for this purpose, with mixed results depending on the practitioner, the dosage, and the context.

Even if they are legal in your area, I don't recommend use of such substances for beginning ritual practitioners. For one thing, it can be easy to mistake a "high" for the ritual state, and they are often not at all the same things. For another, a solid condition of sound mental health is a must before engaging in such exploration. Experiences of altered consciousness can have profound impact on the user.

Finally, generally speaking, less is more when it comes to ritual use of these substances: too much destroys focus and makes achievement of the flow state impossible.

There is not space in this volume to explore how these substances may enhance, impair, or transform ritual experiences. But caution is the watchword: because some of these substances render users emotionally open in a similar manner to ritual trance, users can be psychologically injured by negative experiences.

## Considerations When Planning Group Rituals

If you're planning a ritual for more people than just yourself, you follow a similar planning process to planning a solo ritual, while adding some additional considerations:

- *How many participants will there be?*
  Practically speaking, does the ritual concept work for that many people? What if fewer or more show up—can the ritual accommodate that?

- *How will participants be kept busy during the ritual?*
  Rituals work best when there is a minimum of standing around watching others do something. Give participants things to do.

- *Are the participants' comfort and accommodation considered?*
  Are any participants differently abled in any way? Are you asking them to do things that some may not be able to do, such as to remain on their feet for too long? Be considerate of your participants and their needs.

- *How will you engage their senses? Does the ritual impact participants on multiple sensory levels?*
  Will you share food and drink? If so, what? Have you made accommodations for hygiene concerns? Will people need a cup, or a napkin? Health concerns? Age?

- *What are the logistics of the activities you have planned?*
  Are there materials that must be distributed to participants? If so, how will you do that? Will you need something to light a fire or candles with? Will you need a corkscrew? What about separate serving containers and a tray on which to pass a beverage (in the era of a pandemic, *please* do this!)? Go over every step of the ritual logistics to be sure you will have the tools and advanced planning so everything can go smoothly.

- *Consider the ability and comfort level of participants.*
  Some may need to sit, particularly if the ritual lasts longer than fifteen minutes or so. How will the ritual be for people who can't see or hear well? Make sure participants understand that you are considerate of their needs and it's okay for them to use a chair or otherwise take care of themselves, and to ask for help if they need it.

  What are your plans for unexpected weather? If your plan is to do a ritual outdoors, is there an indoor backup? If not, have you warned people to dress in layers and be prepared for cold or rain or snow or blazing heat? I've done some amazing rituals in the rain, but I was certainly glad to have a woolen cloak.

- *How does your ritual concept square with inclusiveness?*
  Did you assume a male and female sex binary (as in, all the women do one thing and all the men something else)? This can be excluding of people who are nonbinary or genderfluid. Are you equating "black and white" with "bad and good?" Are people with various differing levels of physical or mental ability going to be able to participate? Think about what your ritual might look like to people who aren't like you and be considerate.

- *Does the ritual work as a cohesive whole? Are all the elements consistent with the purpose, theme, and the sensory and symbolic associations?*
  Adjust your outline to take these questions into consideration. Recruit others to help you with different parts of the ritual, so it's not a "one-person show."

  And have fun!

## *Example: A Sample Group Ritual*

This is a ritual that was conducted by the Northern California Atheopagan affinity group (also known as the Live Oak Circle) to celebrate the May Day holiday, with its themes of springtime and sensual enjoyment. There were eight of us, but this ritual would probably work for as many as twelve or so. We themed this simple ritual around the topics of agency and consent. It was the first, formative ritual for that group.

PREPARATION

We brought materials: ribbons, a metal ring, a bowl of chocolate chips, and a set of small medallions showing a spreading oak tree—one for each member of the ritual group.

ARRIVAL

Member A led a guided meditation centering us in our bodies and in the joys of spring.

QUALITIES

Member B spoke in call and response (bold) with the rest of the members:

"May we find virtue **with respect, trust, and kindness!**
"The wonders of the universe **delight us with pleasure!**
"We gather in truth, love, life, and beauty **both now and ever more!"**

DECLARATION OF INTENTION

Member C declared, "We enact this rite to celebrate agency, consent, and pleasure within adult relationships of every healthy kind."

WORKING

When this was done, it was time for the *consent* portion of the working:

First, we cleaned our hands with Sani-Wipes; then, we passed a bowl of chocolate chips; each recipient of the bowl would say to the next person in the circle "Would you like the pleasure of chocolate?"

If the person answered yes, we then asked, "May I feed it to you, my sister/brother?" If they answered no, we said,"Thank you," and passed the bowl so the next recipient could take their own chocolate; if yes we fed a chocolate chip to them, and then passed the bowl, where the process was repeated.

When all had eaten, been fed, or passed, we moved to next part of the Working:

Each of us selected a brightly colored length of ribbon about six feet (two meters) long. If they wished (thus, *agency*), each member then declared, "I choose to link myself to this circle," and tied their ribbon onto a central ring suspended from a tree branch.

When we had all tied our ribbons to the ring, we danced briefly in a circle holding the ribbons (rather like a maypole without the pole), singing the common Pagan chant "We Are a Circle."

#### EXPRESSIONS OF GRATITUDE

Each member expressed their gratitude for the newly formed ritual circle and for anything else in their life they felt grateful for.

#### BENEDICTION:

Member D distributed Live Oak medallions to all members, saying, "Welcome to Live Oak Circle!" In unison, the members declared, "We are the Live Oak Circle!"

We then fell to feasting and enjoying the evening with one another. The ritual was complete.

## Considerations for Online Rituals

With the growth of international communities through the internet—and particularly since the COVID-19 pandemic—it has become increasingly common for Pagan groups that are geographically distanced to conduct their rituals online, over online streaming platforms.

While this may sound awkward and unlikely to be emotionally impactful, such rituals can actually be quite meaningful and help to bring people who may not ever have met in person into greater closeness and intimacy.

With that said, there are specialized considerations for online rituals, and techniques that contribute to their success. Here are some recommendations:

### *Streaming of a Common Focus*

When conducting an online ritual, it isn't possible for all participants to see a Focus unless a separate camera is training on one. Construct your Focus for the ritual with symbols that are as universally recognizable as possible. If you are the ritual's leader, log into your video conferencing account twice: once with your phone, pointed at the Focus, and once for yourself with a tablet or laptop. If you "spotlight" the Focus, everyone will be able to see it during the ritual.

### *Simultaneous Candle Lighting*

A common way to commence an online ritual, having each participant light a candle simultaneously brings a sense of sacred space into the spaces of each online participant, and gives a feeling of commonality and connection.

### *Recitation of Qualities with Call-and-Response Repeat*

Because of the variable audio lag in video conferencing, unison speaking or singing is impossible. However, participants can still repeat each named Quality when they hear it, reinforcing its importance in their minds.

### *Readings or Solo Songs*

One solution to the audio lag problem is to designate a featured solo speaker or singer whose audio is streamed to the participants while they mute their microphones. Participants can then sing along and harmonize with the song without creating a cacophony of lagged audio.

Setting an emotional climate can be more challenging when conducting rituals online. It can help for the host to stream a thematically meaningful video from a source such as YouTube or Vimeo, while sharing their screen with participants. Many music videos are deeply evocative and can help to set the mood.

### *Crafting Projects for the Working Phase*

It is helpful to have something hands-on that online ritual participants can involve themselves with, rather than just watching and listening. Various types of crafty activities work well for this; participants bring the materials to the ritual and then assemble them or create the art during the Working phase. An online group I work with weekly frequently does this for our rituals: we have done drawing, haiku, ribbon-braiding and/or knotting, sigil development, and other forms of individual expression which can then be shared with the group. A variety of ritual craft projects are described in the resource materials at the back of the book. Be sure to let your participants know in advance what materials they will need to bring to the ritual to participate.

### *Making Wishes or Shedding Baggage*

It is common in rituals for people to either want to invoke something they would like to bring in their lives or to symbolically cast something they want to be rid of into a fire, moving water, a hole in the ground, etc. To do this in an online ritual, what I have done is have participants write in the video conferencing chat those things they hope to "cast into the fire." After the ritual, I physically print the chat out and burn these wishes in my home cauldron. In this way the participants know that their wishes have been ritually processed, which makes the ritual more psychologically impactful.

### *Sharing Food and Drink Together*

Sharing food and drink in an online ritual is easier than it sounds. Each participant brings something to eat and/or drink during the Gratitude phase of the ritual, there is a short "show and tell" where they show what they have brought on-screen, and then they eat and drink as the Gratitude phase continues. Food and drink can also be something nice to share when the Working phase of a ritual involves some kind of craft project like those described in the appendices: each participant's craft project can be shown along with their food/drink. As with crafting projects, make sure participants know to bring their food and drink with them before logging into the video conference.

## Contending with the Inner Critic

Everyone has an *inner critic:* a voice inside your head that says you're not doing it right, you're embarrassing yourself, and attacks your self-esteem and confidence.

The key to the magic of ritual is the suspension of disbelief and release of the stiffness prescribed by the internal critic's voice of embarrassment and shame. Just as we must do this to play let's-pretend, to enjoy a book or a movie, so must we surrender our critical minds to the moment in order to submerge ourselves in ritual.

Remember: rituals are play, and play is human! Have fun with it and try not to worry about feeling silly. If you must, think of your ritual as a game, like charades. If you give yourself permission to relax and go with the "game," you'll find yourself deriving meaning and value from the ritual even if part of you is scoffing.

If you continue to be plagued by the inner critic, consider some of these techniques:

Assign the voice to a place outside your head, like a chair in the room. Sit it there and ask it to observe quietly and without judgment. When you hear it pipe up, the voice will likely seem to come from that physical direction, and you can hold up your palm to tell it to be still. After a few tries, it is likely that the inner critic voice will be stilled for the rest of your ritual.

Also, acknowledge that the critic thinks it is helping you: it thinks it is protecting you from making a fool of yourself. But whether or not it was once a protector, it has turned into a jailor, and it is time for you to be set free. Thank it for its attention, tell it you're an adult now and can take it from here, and answer (either aloud or internally) "No, thank you," when it tries to chime in.

And with practice, that part of you will eventually quiet.

# Chapter 4
# A Practice for Yourself

Your personal spiritual practice is about what matters to you: the first things you think of when you reflect on what is good in your life. That could be your family, your lover, your career, your community, your home, the process of learning, the beauty of experiences in nature, the feeling of travel and adventure, a cause you advocate for … anything, really, that you find meaningful.

Start by thinking about that: what do I really care about? Jot down words and images that come to mind. Those concepts and images will help to inform your process as you create your first Focus, or altar.

## Creating a Home Focus

A *Focus* is another word for an *altar*—it's a word Atheopagans use because *altar* seems to imply institutional religion, worship, and even sacrifice, and that's not what a Focus is for at all. A Focus is for exactly what it says: focusing attention and evoking meaning.

A home Focus is a location for contemplation in your household. If you want it more private (a personal Focus), you can put it in your bedroom or even a closet or dresser drawer. Or it can be more prominently displayed where you can see it all the time. That's up to you.

A Focus is an arrangement of objects and images that *evoke meanings and stories* for you. Examples for a personal Focus could include a seashell from a wonderful trip to the Caribbean, your grandfather's watch, a picture of your family, a toy from your childhood. The Focus can be as simple or as complex as you like; mine is quite cluttered and has sections devoted to science, nature, community, and mortality/memory/ancestry. There are no rules: with the items you place on your Focus, you create a unique artwork that is an expression of who you are and what you value. When creating your focus, here are some considerations:

### *Aesthetics*

The Focus should delight the eye and intrigue and draw in the viewer. Beauty matters! What colors do you want? What symbols? You might use symbols of the Earth, Sun, and Moon, fresh flowers, beautiful objects from nature, artworks consistent with the Focus themes, etc. Arrange them attractively! If there is a wall behind the Focus surface, you can mount images and artworks on it.

### *Don't Forget about Lighting!*

Candles or oil lamps make a soft, relaxing glow, and the act of lighting them feels like "activating" the Focus and helps to create a sense that it is a living site of activity. If using flame, be sure there is enough clearance above it so that nothing catches on fire.

### *Are There Ritual Tools You Want to Use?*

Your collection of tools may accumulate as you come to perform more rituals, but common examples include chalices, knives, wands, incense burners, mirrors, jewelry that is only worn during rituals, a deck of oracle or tarot cards, or other such practical ritual tools. Those who come from a Pagan tradition may have more of these "occult"-style tools, but they aren't *necessary*—they just add some color and "Oooooo!" factor to a Focus.

PRACTICAL CONSIDERATIONS

Items like matches and extra incense can be stored behind or to the side of the Focus, or in an attractive container such as a wooden box.

USING YOUR FOCUS

Once you have created your personal Focus, *keep it "alive,"* meaning, don't just let it sit. Make it a site of change and activity. Light the candles and/or burn incense regularly. Move things around. Change it with the changing of the seasons. Clean the Focus occasionally to keep dust from accumulating. Speak a short intention or blessing at your Focus each morning before leaving the house.

My Focus is the literal focus of my spiritual activity in my home. It is a comfort to me to see it when I come home, and contemplating its symbols and glowing candles makes it easy for me to enter the focused, present, liminal ritual state, or "trance."

## Daily and Household Rituals

The next step in building a personal spiritual practice is to take some time every day—or every few days, if you can't manage that—to stop doing for a little while, and just *be*. This takes many forms for many people: I know an Atheopagan who insists on a minimum of ten minutes of "Sun time" and ten of "Star time" for herself and her children every day, simply to feel the warmth on their faces and gaze up to the amazing Cosmos. Others may more formally practice meditation, which reduces stress and has many documented health benefits. Some stretch or do yoga poses; some read a poem or two.

The point is to disengage from the task list and feel the fact that you are living, every day. After a while of doing this, you will find you are getting to know yourself better and enjoying life more.

My daily practice happens in two segments, every day: in the morning, when I don't have much time before I need to go to work, I stand before my Focus and breathe deeply for several breaths, to center myself. Then I open my eyes and drink in all the meaningful objects and images, reflecting on the many stories they tell me from my life and about my world. I draw a single tarot card then and reflect on its meaning as a sort of lens on the coming day. Tarot is a rich symbol set which can be useful for sounding out what is going on in the subconscious. As naturalists, however, Atheopagans typically do not believe in divination in the literal sense of "telling the future."

In the evening, I light the two candles on my Focus: one, in the section for *The World*, where I say the words, "The Sacred Earth;" the other, in the section for *The Underworld*, I light saying, "The Honored Dead." Then I sit with my Focus for a while, in darkness save for the candlelight. I reflect on the day: what I enjoyed, what I learned.

What you choose to do for a daily practice will be unique to you. Try out some different approaches to see what feels best and refine what you do as you go.

## Keeping a Personal Practice Going… and Restarting When It Doesn't

We all get busy. And we get demotivated. Sometimes the oh-what-the-hell-is-the-point factor is strong and we may not do our daily practices. Then, having missed a practice, it feels like something has broken, and it's easier just to not do it again. And again. Pretty soon your Focus is gathering dust and you're feeling vaguely guilty about it.

This happens to everyone. Don't worry about it.

Having a spiritual practice isn't about just one more obligation you have to tick off, such as paying the bills or going to the dentist. It's meant to *enhance* your life, to reduce stress, and help you to be happier.

If you miss a little while—even if it's months—know that you can start again. No harm done. Just begin to take that little bit of time for yourself again. You are worth it.

The good thing about the many opportunities for Atheopagan observance and ritual (see chapter 7) is that there is always a new opportunity rolling around to jumpstart a lapsed practice and get back into the groove. If it's been a while since you did something at your Focus, but the full Moon or one of the eight sabbaths is coming up, you can plan a little something for that event and jump right back in.

The main point is to *keep going*. You never stopped; you just had a longish gap between your ritual observances. The next time you pick up a wand or light a candle, or however you conduct your ritual practices, is just the next step in the unbroken chain of your spiritual practice. It's okay if it's small, or brief. It's you reminding yourself what is important to you, and that this ritual stuff feels pretty good, even if it seems a bit awkward.

Most of us succumb to "Dusty Focus Syndrome" now and then. Life gets busy, or we become saddened or depressed and distant from our spirituality. But it's all waiting for us, in any moment, to dive back in and get recharged.

Seize the opportunity presented by that upcoming Moon phase, or that holiday that's just around the corner, to do a little something special. It doesn't have to be grandiose: just a moment out of time to reflect that we are here, tiny beings in a far-flung Universe of treasures and mysteries. We are gifted with Life, and with consciousness. We are each of us unique, precious, and magical.

Mark the passage of the days of this too-short life with gratitude, and you'll find yourself seeing more reasons to be grateful. More reasons to feel love. More reasons to be motivated to add your voice to the chorus of all of us who stand for better, kinder values, and reverence for our Sacred Earth.

## Private Practice vs. Including Family and Friends

You have a right to your own spiritual path. No one can tell you otherwise. If you want your rituals to remain private, by all means, keep them so. Some of us are surrounded by people who actively disapprove of people who have different paths than they do, and if that's you, by all means, keep your practices private if you don't want to provoke conflict.

That said, it can be a source of deep joy, celebration, and fun to celebrate rituals—especially the holidays described later in the book—with loved ones. Many Atheopagan parents share their rituals with their children, although our general ethic is that children must, when they are old enough, be given their own free choices about what spirituality, if any, they want to practice.

Atheopagan rituals, like those described in this book, can be lively, emotionally moving, psychologically powerful, and/or simply fun. Why wouldn't you want to invite loved ones to share in such activities?

However, you are the only one who can make that call. In some cases, it's better just to quietly pursue your own practice. And some rituals are personal, for you only.

If you do invite others to join you, have them help you design and enact the ritual! Rituals are better when there are no spectators, only participants, and collaborative ritual design is a fun process. See later chapters on occasions for celebrating rituals, for examples of the kinds of things you can do with a group, and for tips on recruiting and cultivating community you can share your ritual observances with.

# Chapter 5
# Ritual Skills

A *ritualist* is someone who leads or conducts rituals. As we have seen, rituals are symbolic actions taken to effect change in our consciousness, emotions, confidence, beliefs, or life experience.

Being an effective ritualist, particularly as a leader of group rituals, is about both leadership and the development of ritual skills, which enable you to shape your own emotions and those of co-participants. Master them, and you will not only find your rituals to be impactful and memorable, but you will also become more comfortable and confident in leading groups, which can be helpful in all kinds of life situations. But there are some general recommendations I can make before going into the specifics of ritual skills we can work to develop so our rituals have more emotional impact.

The first general rule-of-thumb for ritual leadership—whether by yourself or with others—is *confidence.* Even if the voice in your head is shouting that you are an impostor, you should project supreme assuredness in your demeanor and body language, because such a stance will both communicate to others and help you yourself to be confident in your ritual's effectiveness. So speak boldly and stand proudly! Model a sense of freedom within the ritual circle and remember that emotional openness and vulnerability are far more important than a polished performance.

The next general rule is *preparation.* Sometimes rituals have many moving parts and you need to walk yourself through the steps a few times to ensure you are ready to perform them as planned. If you need to light something on fire, where are the matches or lighter? If you need to pour wine, do you have a corkscrew, or have you opened the bottle in advance and lightly corked it so you can easily open it by hand? If there is a poem to be read, where is it? What is the light source you will use to read it? All of these details must be addressed in order for your ritual to flow smoothly.

Finally, for presentational elements of your rituals, you will need to practice. Is there a song you will sing, or a speech you will make? Practice them: it will improve your confidence and the quality of your performance in the actual ritual.

## Specific Ritual Skills

When you do rituals by yourself, the most important ritual skill is the ability to enter the ritual state, which is sometimes called *trance* or *flow*. Creating that mental space of openness, vulnerability, and presence in the moment is a skill, and with time it can become easier. See page 23 for information about how to enter the ritual state.

Now, if you are a solitary practitioner, all you need to conduct rituals are privacy, the ability to open yourself to the ritual state, and the confidence to carry yourself through your ritual process.

If you plan to enact rituals with other people, however, there are some core skills that it would really help to master. These skills can help your rituals to feel energetic, alive, and compelling. These skills are Public Speaking and Storytelling, Singing, Drumming and Rhythm, and Movement. You will find that cultivating skill in these areas will contribute overall to your enjoyment in life, even if you are solitary.

## *Public Speaking and Storytelling*

Speaking before an audience is terrifying for many people. In fact, surveys indicate that many fear public speaking more than death itself.

However, for ritualists, speaking confidently before a group of listeners is a core skill that enables clear communication, evocation of emotion, and establishment of leadership credibility, which can inspire a sense of safety and confidence in the ritual proceedings.

As a ritual leader, your spoken voice is perhaps your most powerful tool for moving participants into ritual space and common purpose. As a participant, your voice is sure to be called upon at times to invoke the qualities that you hope to bring into the circle, or to express your gratitude for good things in your life. And in community, in or out of circle, speaking your truth is essential: it is how we remain truly *with* one another. As feminist Maggie Kuhn has it, "speak the truth, even if your voice shakes."[6]

I am fortunate in that public speaking has always been easy for me; I know that for many, it is a tremendous challenge. Here are some pointers that I hope can help you to be a more effective ritual and community speaker:

### AVOID MEMORIZING SPEECHES

If at all possible—that is, unless the wording has to be exact for some reason—do not attempt to memorize a speech. There is too much that can go wrong with a memorized speech. You might lose track and forget the next part of what you are saying, or the presentation can appear wooden and lifeless because you are regurgitating something from memory and focusing on recall rather than connecting with listeners. Short passages are okay for memorization, but it is much better to work from a short set of talking points and speaking spontaneously about each of these. The talking points can be memorized, or you can keep a small card in your hand listing them as a reminder. A poem or quotation may be read from

6. "Maggie Kuhn," National Women's Hall of Fame, accessed November 6, 2023, https://www.womenofthehall.org/inductee/maggie-kuhn/.

paper, but it's much better to read from a book or binder, as loose pages can flop all over the place.

### IF NECESSARY, SPEAK FROM TALKING POINTS

If you have too much material to be summarized by a brief set of talking points, consider dividing up the material and having more than one person deliver it. Variety helps listeners to maintain focus, and it's much better to have two people speaking from talking points rather than one reading from pages.

### OTHER THAN AS NOTED, DON'T READ A SPEECH FROM PAPER OR CUE CARDS

This is the surest way to kill the energy of a ritual circle. Reading from a page can appear flat and devitalized, and especially under low light conditions (recommended for most rituals, as it contributes to entry into the ritual state), readers are sure to stumble over written text. The alternative is that you may be juggling a flashlight (tip: use a headlamp) along with pages of text, and the flow and confidence that are necessary for ritual leadership just become impossible. Staring at a page prevents connection with listeners, and is an immediate boredom cue for them. A key part of what establishes leadership is the sense from participants that you are confident in yourself and what you are saying.

### PRACTICE

If you are not confident in your public speaking abilities, practice speaking from your talking points until you feel better about what you will present. The speech doesn't have to come out the same way every time; after all, the listeners don't even know what the talking points are. Practicing before a mirror will help you with confident posture and looking (yourself) in the eye while speaking.

### SPEAK TO YOUR AUDIENCE

Look them in the eye (or, if that's too hard, look them in the forehead, which is a trick that looks like you're looking them in the eye). Connecting with listeners is the surest way for them to know that your words are sincere and are meant for them. Think of your speech as a conversation: the attention and feedback you get from listeners is their response. Feel free to ask questions in case you're explaining something that may not be clear.

### IF YOU MAKE A MISTAKE, CARRY ON

Everyone makes mistakes. You can make a joke about it, or just keep going.

### DO RELAXING EXERCISES BEFORE YOU NEED TO SPEAK

Take some deep breaths. Remind yourself that you know how to do this, that you have what it takes. Use the grounding techniques described starting on page 213. Be in your body and ready to step forward in confidence.

### LEARN TO PROJECT YOUR VOICE

Particularly for women (as higher-pitched voices tend not to carry as far), this is essential for any but the smallest ritual contexts. Learn to tell the difference between projection (speaking from the diaphragm) and yelling (speaking loudly through the vocal chords, which strains the voice quickly).

### EMOTION IS GOOD

Listeners want to see your passion for the subject. Show them. *Remember: listeners in ritual circle are on your side!* They're not there to criticize you or find fault with your presentation; they want to go where you want to lead them. Think of yourself as among friends when speaking in circle.

---

*The ritual circle is intended as a safe container.* When we form in a circle for a ritual, it is to say that what happens within occurs in a context of trust, cooperation, and amicability. Your speech does not have to be perfect to be great or effective.

Our abilities with language are a major element of what makes us unique as humans. We are able to communicate complex and subtle ideas and emotions through the power of the voice. Claim yours as an essential component of your power: your rituals and your community will be the stronger for it.

## *Storytelling*

Much of the speaking that happens in ritual circles is storytelling. There are some special considerations when telling a story, though most of the public speaking recommendations still apply. You may not be able to learn an entire story and tell it by heart. You may have to read it. If you do, here are some tips:

### MAKE SURE YOU HAVE A GOOD LIGHT SOURCE

A headlamp is preferable to a flashlight, as juggling pages with a flashlight can be awkward. Or, though I tend not to like using technological tools in rituals, a backlit tablet can be a useful way to go. Remember your audience and engage them with as much eye contact as possible

Don't "hide in the text"—look up often and especially when dramatic events are happening in the story. Try to read ahead a little so you know what is coming next.

### EMOTION IS ESPECIALLY IMPORTANT IN STORYTELLING

What are the characters feeling? How can you communicate that with your voice?

### USE DIFFERENT VOICES FOR DIFFERENT CHARACTERS

It can be hard to tell who is talking in a story sometimes—make it easier for listeners by using different vocal registers or accents.

ACT OUT THE STORY WITH YOUR BODY

Even holding pages or a tablet, you can indicate characteristics and events through body movement. Your listeners will appreciate it!

AGAIN, PRACTICE

It is especially important to practice telling a story. Getting the timing, the dramatic beats, the volume dynamics worked out will make your story really compelling.

## *Singing*

Singing is a core skill for the ritual practitioner. You don't have to be a professional-quality singer, but you need to be able to sing a tone, at least, and better, to be able to sing a melody with reasonable accuracy. Especially if you're going to be working in a group.

Singing requires deep breathing. It engages the body and the brain's limbic system, where emotion and social connection are centered, and tends to help disengage the thinking mind. In other words, it helps participants to enter the ritual state.

When people sing together, their breathing synchronizes. Even their brain waves synch up. Singing together is a way of creating something of a group mind—a collective entity larger than the individuals within it.

Singing is creative. For those who are able to harmonize, even a chant repeated over and over can be an endless opportunity for creative variation. Harmony adds to the evocative richness of music, to its beauty and emotional power.

Repetition, too, can help to evoke the ritual state. Pagan ritual chants tend to be repeated, but good ones somehow never become boring. Instead, the experience of singing them—particularly as a part of a group—simply leads to deeper and deeper entrainment, emotional openness, and joy. Harmonies emerge.

For those of us who aren't accustomed to singing, I can't emphasize enough how important it is to start. Yes, it feels awkward at first, and you may be shy about it. However, if you hope to lead rituals with other people, it is a skill you will deeply value.

Start in as easy a manner as you can. Sing in the shower. Play music you love in the car and sing along. If nothing else, you can hum while doing your personal rituals at your Focus. Anything that helps you to become more comfortable as a person who sings will serve you well in your ritual practice.

Here is a simple chant I wrote that you can practice singing, and can use in your rituals if you like:

*Green earth below*
*Bright sky above*
*Let me live*
*My life for love*

### Drumming and Rhythm

The first musical instrument was almost certainly something resonant being struck: a hollow log, a stalagmite in a cave. In fact, percussive rhythm may predate humans as a species: monkeys have been observed beating on hollow logs in a call-and-response with other monkeys. Certainly the noises made while pounding seeds and roots into meal would naturally have become a source of play, even for pre-humans.

Despite this near certainty, we don't have any fossil evidence of Paleolithic drums. Only flutes, because they were made of bone and could survive over tens of thousands of years. Still, in every culture of the world, we find percussive instruments, and with them, percussive play—often in a context of religious ceremony.

Drumming and the experience of rhythm is viscerally impactful upon human emotions. Rhythm stirs a desire to move, and it is no surprise that one of the most mysterious and yet joyful of human activities, **dancing,** relies heavily on rhythm.

Rhythm is a deeply effective ritual technology. Striking up a beat encourages ritual celebrants to participate with their bodies, not just their minds. Even a simple, steady "heartbeat drum" can have profound effect on the atmosphere of a ritual, creating a sense of solemnity and foreboding.

Rhythmic sounds—drumming, rattling and other percussion—are helpful in bringing celebrants into *entrainment,* which is defined as synchronization of participants with an external rhythm, accomplished through repetition. Drumming and rattling are common means to the *entrainment* of a group creating a ritual. In a broader sense, however, entrainment means getting all participants "on the same page," or moving in the same direction: to create a shared state in which they can express, celebrate and act together. Entrainment is a critically important aspect of successful group ritual; when true entrainment has happened, you can feel that the ritual is really cooking.

I encourage you to master, at the very least, some simple rhythmic percussion for purposes of stirring up and maintaining **energy** during rituals. And let your fellow participants help! It's great to have a basket of rattles, shakers, claves, chimes, and other rhythmic noisemakers for participants to borrow so they can participate in the soundscape of your ritual. Drumming can be particularly powerful during the Working segment of a ritual.

Recorded music can also be effective in creating a "groove and vibe" for your ritual—perhaps trance-y, spacey music or sounds from nature at the Arrival segment to contribute to participants entering the ritual state, and then more rhythmic and driving music during the Working phase of the ritual. The downside of using recorded music is that you don't have as much control over the tempo, volume, and duration of the sound as you do when creating the music yourself. However, if you practice with your recorded music, you should be able to guide the feeling of your ritual well.

To me, it feels better that the sounds for a ritual be generated there, by its participants, rather than reproduced electronically. Still, when doing solo or very small group rituals, you may not have free hands for drumming, and recorded music may be best. Suggestions for various kinds of recorded ritual music are listed in the resources at the end of the book.

Drumming and rhythm are powerful gateways to the ritual state. Learning to master even simple drum rhythms will be powerful additions to your toolbox as you learn to conduct rituals.

### *Movement and Dance*

Since probably before humans were even human, there has been music; rhythm, at least. And where there is rhythm, there is dance. There are preserved footprints in painted caves in France that indicate young boys dancing 20,000 to 30,000 years ago.[7] Some ritual dances are still performed today, after untold continuous centuries.

*Ritual isn't just something that happens in our heads.* When effective, it is an immersive experience, involving our entire beings. We are not, after all, just brains carried by flesh robots; our nervous systems extend throughout our bodies and participate heavily in our brain states.

Effective rituals involve some kind of engagement of the body: **singing,** for example, or clapping, dancing, walking, or other movement to music or rhythm.

There is good reason for this. Stimulating the metabolism through exercise, especially in a creative, expressive form such as dance or music-making, is deeply pleasurable and requires that the participant be present in the limbic ritual state. There is a reason why we are drawn to these activities: they are joyful, even when solemn. They enhance our lives' happiness.

I'm a pretty heady person, myself. I feel awkward, and it's hard for me to let myself go and dance (but when I do, it feels like flying!). But I can say with confidence that the most powerful and joyful rituals I have done have all involved some kind of physical exertion, even if it is simply in the form of **walking or dancing free form about a fire,** singing and feeling my body's aliveness.

Incorporating movement into ritual can be challenging, because participants can be self-conscious and not want to go first. **Lower light conditions** reduce this, so firelight or candlelight or moonlight will help (there

7. Clottes, Jean. "Chauvet Cave (ca. 30,000 B.C.)." In *Heilbrunn Timeline of Art History*. New York: The Metropolitan Museum of Art, 2000–.

is a reason why dance clubs are dark). As a ritual leader, however, never forget that you are setting the standard for what is "normal" in the circle. Participants are looking to you to see how to behave. Therefore, when it's time to move, *move!* Push yourself to overcome any shyness you may feel so others feel "permission" to let go and move themselves.

You can also start slowly, with swaying, perhaps, and raising the arms, and as the musical intensity increases, so does the movement.

Music contains all shades of emotion, so if you use recorded music as well as rhythm, choose carefully. Even better is to have one or more musicians as a part of your ritual, so they can work with the **ritual atmosphere or energy** in an organic manner.

Be sure to work with movement in an arc: start slower, build up, and then direct where that energy goes, be it into a final joyous tone sung to the sky, or slowing down again until participants are still and silent. There are plenty of possibilities, but don't just let things go until they peter out: take them somewhere deliberate.

Movement and rhythm—the engagement of the body—are the parts of ritual that may be most unfamiliar and uncomfortable for those who come to experience it for the first time.

The point of ritual is to *get beyond thinking.* Spirituality isn't just philosophy: it's a practice. It is accomplished in the doing. If you or some of your participants, like me, tend to lead with their thinking minds, just know that it is intensely liberating to finally let the thinking go for a while, to *move,* and be *alive.*

# Chapter 6
# Ritual Arts

This section presents a variety of artistic ritual activities that can be folded into your celebrations of personal, cyclical, healing, and rite of passage rituals. They are derived from Pagan spellcraft activities and are psychologically impactful when incorporated into ritual observances.

Ritual is a form of play—even when it is solemn, it is imaginative and creative. These activities' artistic nature can help us to enter the trancelike ritual state of consciousness.

## On Cultural Appropriation

Just because you like the look of art or ritual techniques from other cultures—particularly Indigenous cultures which exist today—does not mean you have the right to use them. This is a hard concept for some of us living under capitalism to understand; after all, we are accustomed to feeling "entitled" to anything we can afford to pay for.

But this is not the way of many of Earth's diverse cultures. And Indigenous people, particularly, have suffered so much under colonialism that it is an exploitative insult simply to steal their spiritual traditions, symbols, art works, etc., for your own ritual work unless you have been explicitly given permission to do so by someone who has the authority to grant this permission from their culture.

Today, we see the phenomenon of what Indigenous people call "plastic shamans:" white practitioners who offer apparently native spiritual experiences or training, such as sweat lodge ceremonies, without having any such permission or training from the cultures they are stealing from. This is wrong, and, ethically speaking, it must be avoided.

Practices like singing, telling stories, dancing and drumming belong to all of us: they extend far back into prehistoric times and are found in cultures throughout the world. You can do enough with these and the ritual arts listed here without horning in on cultures which have already seen so much exploitation and oppression at the hands of non-native colonialists.

This said, let's look at some of the many practices we can fold into our rituals:

## Gathering Materials and Making Implements

Nature provides abundant materials that can be used in rituals. Sometimes completely unaltered materials may be evocative of the purpose for a ritual, as when using holly or conifer cones to suggest the Midwinter holiday.

In other cases, items gathered from nature may be used as materials for crafting ritual symbols and tools. This section contains some suggestions.

Materials can also be gathered at the time of events, which make them special. Saving some rain from a big storm, or sitting water out in the moonlight on the night of a full Moon, for example, can give a feeling of specialness to the water that you can then incorporate into your rituals.

There are ethical considerations relating to gathering ritual materials. In most cases, remember that "dead or shed" is a good rule for deciding which materials are okay to gather from nature. *Do not* peel bark or cut branches from living trees—instead, use fallen branches and their bark. Be considerate of the impacts of your collecting and make an effort not to disturb habitat for wild animals such as insects, arachnids, and small mammals.

Seashells, leaves, feathers, seed pods, flowers, tree bark, found bones or antlers, sticks and rocks can all be used as symbols when creating rituals, or crafted into tools such as wands and incense burners. Be aware that gathering such materials is illegal in many parks, and possession of some wildlife body parts—even if collected from dead animals—is prohibited. Make sure to be cognizant of pertinent laws and make your material collecting choices accordingly.

## Guided Meditations

A guided meditation is a staple of many rituals. This is a "journey inside the mind" where a narrator leads the participants to have an experience, rather like being in a story.

A guided meditation is typically written in advance in order to ensure that all the symbolic and meaningful elements desired have been incorporated. It is usually formatted as a *voyage:* a journey to go to a place (real or imagined), have an experience that imparts wisdom, learning, or empowerment, and then (in most cases) a return to reach the normal world and the place where the participant is laying or sitting.

Begin your guided meditation by inviting participants to get comfortable and to close their eyes if comfortable with doing so; if not, eyes may be half-closed so they experience only dimly lit vision. Meditative music or a slow drumbeat can help to facilitate the participants' experience.

Next should come a progressive series of relaxation instructions: *breathe deeply, feeling a calm awareness spread through your body from your chest out to the very tips of your fingers and toes. Feel your consciousness falling, now, dropping softly until, nearly weightless, you are floating on a cushion of warm air.* Note that these instructions are in the second person ("you"); guided meditations should always be in this tense. Take your time—make sure participants are given a chance to truly relax into a light trance state.

Once the participants are relaxed and ready to "travel," tell them what they are seeing, feeling, smelling, and hearing with vivid descriptions. *You become aware that you are in a deep forest, walking along a narrow path. Light filters dimly through the tall trees and you can smell the rich combination of damp soil and pine. It is nearly silent; only a tiny sigh of wind in the treetops reaches your ears other than the soft pad of your footfalls on the path.* Use a calm, melodious tone of voice.

As the voyage progresses, continue describing what the participants are experiencing, leading to the destination. This can be anything: a garden, a cave containing a dragon, a hollow tree leading to a fairy glen—anything you can imagine that makes sense for the meaning you are working to impart to participants.

There, the participants typically either witness a symbolic event, or meet a Wise One or Wise Ones: sources of wisdom and knowledge. Again, this can be anything you imagine: A historical figure, a Being of Light (or Darkness), a god or goddess, a fierce monster like a dragon, and so forth. This figure may say something, present a gift, or anything else you think is appropriate. It is often best to have the participant fill in for themselves what the gift or statement is—that way, the offering is selected by the participant's own subconscious and it will be exactly tailored to what the participant needs. You can ask questions that the participants fill in for themselves, too: *What do they tell you? What do you see in the box?*

Next comes the return voyage. This shouldn't be as detailed as the original voyage. I like to use a zoom out effect so the participants' perspective pulls out, the scene growing smaller and smaller as they rise up into the sky, until clouds obscure the scene and they find themselves back in the room, seated or laying where they are. You instruct that when ready, they should open their eyes. "Flying up through an underground tunnel" is another popular choice.

The guided meditation is a powerful technique, and an exceedingly flexible one. You can use it with individuals or with a group of one hundred (just make sure they can hear you; you may need amplification). The voyage can be through any kind of real or imagined landscape, with any kind of destination or wise guide. Learning to lead an effective guided meditation is a valuable skill for a leader of group rituals.

See page 213 for some examples of guided meditations. Many more are available on the Internet, including recorded guided meditations that you can use yourself for inner voyaging.

## First-Person Voyaging Rituals

Throughout history, practitioners of many cultures have used ritual techniques to enter a trance and take "voyages" in their minds. These voyages can involve encountering and communicating with spirits, magical animals, and other powerful psychological figures, the nature of which varies widely depending on the culture of the voyaging practitioner. They can be done solo, or with other practitioners providing support like drumming, chanting, playing instruments or singing.

Sometimes these practitioners take co-ritualists with them by describing what they see as it happens or "report back" on what they have experienced after their return to a normal, lucid state. What is brought back by the practitioner usually includes messages for the subject of the ritual, which might be for the practitioner themself if the voyaging is a solitary ritual or may be for a person who is suffering some kind of malady, or it may be for the entire community. In the case of a voyage to seek aid in healing, these messages may prescribe further ritual actions or medical recommendations; when voyaging for the community, messages may include advice or warnings.

These techniques are quite similar to the guided visualization technique I described previously, but in this case the ritual leader is spontaneously experiencing the events of the voyage in real time, rather than the participants being led through a pre-written experience. To be good at this technique a practitioner needs to have a very strong grasp of entering and staying in the ritual state, even if surprised or interrupted by activities around them or by a shocking vision.

While Western anthropologists adopted a Tunguskan word, *shaman*, to describe such ritual leaders, many Indigenous people object to the wholesale characterization of individual cultures with a single term. I prefer to think of the generic, non-culturally specific technique I describe here as *first-person voyaging.*

Conducting a first-person voyage requires skill, practice, and preparation. The practitioner may wish to dress in special clothing created specifically for ritual activities, for example. Optimally, the practitioner makes this clothing themselves, adding symbols, sewing in sacred objects that they find meaningful, and so forth. Alternatively, the practitioner may have special jewelry like a necklace or bracelets that they don for purposes of first-person voyaging. Some voyagers also choose to fast on the day of their voyage, which can help the voyager to be a bit light-headed and make it easier to enter a trance.

## *Example: First-Person Voyage*

The setting for such a voyage should be particularly safe and secure. If done in a home, for example, it may be a good idea to have a guardian stationed outside the door to prevent any unexpected interruptions.

### ARRIVAL PHASE

Arrival for a first-person voyage should create as magical an environment as possible. This can include smoke blessing, asperging with sacred water, wine, or other liquid, setting up a Focus with ritual tools and symbols, and/or other ritual steps to sacralize the space and contribute to the imagery and trance of the voyager. Drawing a "magic circle" around the space or applying a ritual "sealing" to the entrance may be a part of this consecration of the ritual working space.

Drumming, rattling, and rhythmic percussive music are commonly used to contribute to the voyager's trance. The voyager may drum or use a rattle or other percussion instrument, or the other participants in the ritual may provide sound through drumming, chanting, or singing. Recorded music (see the list of recommended ritual music in the appendix) may also be used, but it should be managed by someone other than the voyager, whose responsibility it will be to watch carefully to see when to turn the music up, down, or off.

INVOCATION OF QUALITIES

This phase should list a broad range of qualities, animals, plants, ancestors, even deities, so whatever characteristics and imagery show up in the voyage have been invited to do so.

THE WORKING/VOYAGE PHASE

- **Non-voyaging participants (if any):** Give the voyager plenty of room to move, as they may wish to move around or even dance wildly (conversely, they may want to lay down while voyaging—depends on the individual). Other practitioners surround the voyager, and may participate as drummers, singers/chanters, or simple witnesses if the voyager directs that others be silent so as not to interrupt their experience. If the ritual is for purposes of healing, the participants should circle closely around the healing subject so that the sound of their drums, rattles or voices washes over them.
- **Voyager:** Begin by closing your eyes and concentrating on the sounds of the drummers or singers If solitary, you can drum yourself to enter trance if you are experienced with this way of entering the ritual state; if not, you can use recorded music. Breathe deeply. If you want to move to the music, move freely within the space provided. If you are indoors, gaze at a section of wall. Visualize that wall dissolving, opening into a dark space beyond that you fly forward into. You may enter a tunnel, or a dark open space, or you may be flying through outer space or above a vast forest—there are infinite possibilities. Your voyage has begun.

If you are outdoors, you may visualize a tunnel opening in the Earth leading to a subterranean realm, or a giant plant bursting through the ground and growing toward the sky, which you can climb to an upper realm, or you may see yourself rising up into the air to encounter your messengers. Again, the possibilities are limited only by your imagination.

After initiating the voyage, ask (either internally or aloud), "What do you need to show me?" The symbols and characters of your voyage will begin to appear. You can speak to them, ask them questions.

When you wish to return, say "return" aloud three times. This will pull your consciousness back from its trance voyage to the physical locality where the ritual is taking place.

After the return, the voyager may want to take a few minutes to organize their thoughts about their experience. Then, if they are working in a group, they report the events and meanings of their experience, describing what they have learned for the participants and/or subject of the ritual.

Note that sometimes, other participants may go into trance and have experiences as well! If the participant(s) wish, these may be reported after the voyager describes what they have learned.

### GRATITUDE PHASE

This phase is very important in these voyaging rituals. The voyager should thank all of the Qualities invoked at the beginning of the ritual, and particularly each of those characters and symbols encountered in the voyage for their wisdom and knowledge. The gratitude of fellow participants should be expressed as well. Remember, you are thanking your own deep wisdom and perspicacity: be kind and gracious with yourselves.

### BENEDICTION

The Benediction phase is a firm declaration that the ritual has concluded. The "magic circle" is undone or the "seal" is removed from the door; if indoors, you may want to open all the windows to "let the world in." Just be sure that it is made very clear to all participants that the ritual space is now dismissed and the ordinary world's conditions now reign.

### POST-RITUAL

It is very important to re-ground all participants, and particularly the voyager, in normal reality. Because trance can be so otherworldly, it can be dangerous to operate heavy machinery or perform other hazardous tasks when not completely "reawakened" from the state of trance. Eating food with complex carbohydrates or protein and drinking a full glass of water helps with this a great deal, and a shared meal provides an opportunity to discuss the messages received. Placing the soles of their bare feet against the Earth is another valuable grounding technique often used by voyagers.

First-person voyaging can be a very powerful form of ritual practice for engaging your subconscious knowledge—this knowledge can help you to understand yourself and your life better, and even warn you about possible dangers. I recommend it be taken up after you are proficient in entering the ritual state of trance and know your way around how to work in ritual spaces.

### *Important Reminder*

As previously noted, there are many promulgators of supposed "shamanic" techniques who directly steal cultural practices from Indigenous traditions without permission, training, or approval of the people whose practices they are attempting to imitate, and often for money. This is deeply unethical and in the case of commercial transactions constitutes literal theft of much-needed resources from Indigenous practitioners.

What is described here is a "generic" voyaging technique not sourced from any particular culture and bearing commonalities with many, past and present. We have examples going back many thousands of years which show that such voyaging has taken place in many cultures throughout the world, including Western ones such as the ancient Oracle at Delphi. *It is not appropriate, valid or necessary for such voyaging practices to appropriate symbols, songs, practice elements or design elements from Indigenous cultures living today.*

## Candle Rituals

Candles provide a romantic, magical atmosphere for many reasons. Low light conditions tend to provoke a spooky desire on the part of people to be quieter, possibly as a result of our roots as diurnal animals afraid of nocturnal predators. Flickering golden light provides a soft, hushed ambience that works perfectly on a **Focus** and which is conducive to the ritual state, which is why they feature so prominently in the altar spaces of pretty much every religion on Earth. And after all, lighting candles is a rather "magical" act, in that it creates dancing heat and light out of (apparently) nothing.

Here are steps you can take to "consecrate" your candle or candles to the ritual purpose you intend. Remember that you will want to concentrate on your goal for your ritual throughout these activities. When selecting and preparing a candle for ritual, here are some considerations:

### *Safety*

First, consider fire safety. Dangling sleeves or proximity of highly flammable materials are not appropriate for working with fire. Make sure you have a fire extinguisher or bucket of water available to douse a fire if one gets started, and be smart about what kinds of objects and materials you place in proximity to fire.

### *Color*

Choose the color for your ritual candle based on what kind of intention you have for your ritual and what color you find best associated with that goal. If your ritual goal is a complex one, you may want to use more than one candle, of differing colors. Note that there are no inherent meanings to colors; what matters is what the candle color means to you.

### *Scent*

Personally, I don't care for scented candles, preferring to use essential oils or incense independently to create the scent experience for my rituals. However, tastes vary, and you may want to use a candle with a particular scent that is meaningful to you as a part of your ritual.

### *Inscription*

Carving a word, a symbol or sigil (see page 84) into a candle is another way to charge it with associations for your ritual purposes. If you have one, use a **ritual knife,** or a special knife you have ritually consecrated to the purpose.

### *Anointing*

Dressing a candle with scented or "blessed" oil is a common way of making a candle special and unique. Choose a scent that you associate with your ritual intent: if your purpose is passionate, you might use a spicy oil such as carnation, juniper or yew, or even cinnamon. Other scents may strike you as calming, or dreamy, or energizing, or associated with a particular memory. Rub the oil up and down the candle until a smooth, even coating is applied throughout.

### *Smoke Blessing*

In additional or alternatively, you can pass a candle through smoke from burning incense, herbs, or leaves. Choose those that reflect the associations with which you want to imbue the ritual candle (but be certain that you avoid burning toxic leaves such as hemlock, camphor, oleander, etc.) You can also roll an oiled candle in powdered herbs so they will burn along with the candle; if you do, be sure to put the candle in a dish or holder to burn, as burning herbs may fall off the candle and you want to be mindful of safety.

### *Ritual Lighting*

Lighting a ritual candle can be the moment of "igniting" the power of the ritual, or there can be further steps. To me, it is more powerful and evocative to light a candle with a wooden, strike-anywhere match than with a lighter. Speak your intention as an invocation over the candle as you light it.

### *Wax Sealing*

After your candle is lit, you may want to use it to create a "spell note." This is done by writing your ritual intention as a phrase on a small square of paper of the same color as your candle. Then fold each of the corners of the square into the center of the square, resulting in a smaller square. Glue the points of the paper down by dripping wax from your candle to form a seal, hiding and "locking in" the ritual's intention. You can add to the sense of "sealing" and ritual by impressing a signet ring, envelope seal, or other textured item into the candle wax. The sachet can go on your Focus to remind you of your intention, or you can bury it, hang it in a tree or otherwise "offer it to nature." You can use actual sealing wax for this same function, but if you're burning a ceremonial candle anyway, it will integrate well to use the wax from it to "seal the magic" into your intention sachet. Note that sealing wax melts at a much higher temperature than candle wax, and avoid burning yourself by making contact with it.

### *Ceromancy*

This is a form of **divination** (see page 83) using the shapes formed by wax as it is dripped from a burning candle into water. Prepare yourself by meditating or contemplating your candle's flame until you feel calm and centered. Then drip wax into a bowl or chalice of cold water. Look for shapes that form; our brains' propensity for pattern recognition causes us to see recognizable forms in such random stimuli. Look for symbols, objects or animals: what do they mean to you? How does that meaning relate to your life at this time?

---

Candle rituals can be impactful, meaningful… and fun! Give one a try as a part of your ritual practice and see how it works for you. Don't forget the most important part of every ritual: acting in accordance with your intention for the ritual *after* it is completed!

## Knot Rituals

There has long been a sort of magic associated with textiles and cordage. Knitting, crocheting, and other textile crafts miraculously fabricate garments and other useful items out of simple yarn. And many disciplines, like sailing, have specialized knots that in past times were considered secrets of their trades.

### *Sample: Storing Emotion*

Following is a simple knot magic activity that can be used as the Working for a ritual intended to store increments of some emotion or Quality for release later, as with a battery, when the user needs it.

#### You will need

Three differently colored lengths of ribbon or heavy yarn. Pick colors that relate in your mind to the Quality you with which you will imbue your knots.

PROCESS

At the proper point in the ritual, take up your three ribbons, concentrating on the Quality (like courage, confidence, patience, or strength) you want to "capture" into them. Braid the three strands together, tying off each end of the completed braid.

Then, repeating, "I bind (Quality) into these knots," tie several overhand knots (half-hitches) into the braid.

Keep the knotted braid on your Focus. When you have occasion to need the Quality "bound into" the knotted braid, take it in both hands, take a deep breath, concentrate and untie one of the overhand knots. Imagine the Quality entering your body and mind.

When all the knots have been used, you can "recharge" the braid by repeating the ritual and tying new knots into it.

## Potions

The potion is a staple of stereotypical ritual "magic" and witchcraft, and potions of various kinds are easy to make. Most potions are made in the Working phase of a ritual, so you can focus your intended meaning and purpose into the potion you are creating. Here are some considerations and instructions for working with potions.

### *Safety*

Don't drink potions unless you are certain that all ingredients in your potion are safe! Use them to anoint (daub) ritual tools, to pour libations, and for other ritual activities, but do not drink them. Also, be smart: don't use toxic materials like bleach or ammonia, which can react with other ingredients to create poisonous gasses. If you insert a paper with a sigil (see page 84) into your potion, use a regular pencil to draw the sigil. Graphite (pencil "lead") is not real lead, and is harmless. Remember that your potion will, sooner or later, go back into the Earth. Be responsible.

### *Considerations*

While a potion can be made with any liquid (typically water, liquor, or wine) and any added solid ingredients, there are aspects you may want to think about.

What color would you like for it to be? You can get red with a slice of beet or by boiling your water with red cabbage; green with some chopped mint. Yellow onion skins make a nice orange/yellow, especially if you add some vinegar to the potion. In a pinch, you can use food-grade coloring for colors you can't generate naturally. Be aware that most colors will eventually degrade.

What are the meaningful additives you can include that will make the potion mean what you want? Are there stones, herbs, items from nature, symbols that will help? Many edible herbs can be made into a tea infusion and consumed. Be creative: one historical example of "protective magic" involved putting pins, needles, and nails into a jar of the maker's own urine, and then burying it!

What are you going to do with it? Seal the container as a "spell jar" and sit it on a shelf? Bury it? Place it in a special place? Pour it out as a libation? Give it as a gift, symbolizing the meaning you focused on in the ritual where you made the potion?

Or, is it to be drunk? Typically, these are teas ("infusions"), or wine- or liquor-based potions ("elixirs"), made with *edible* plants. A quiet moment sipping a potion you have created with intention can be a real psychological boost.

## *Making a Potion*

In almost all circumstances, I recommend starting with a base of water, but as in the cases described, you can use wine or liquor. Even better, it's good to use *special* water: gathered from a beloved river or stream, or captured during a downpour, or "charged" by sitting out all night in the moonlight. The "specialness" contributes to the otherworldly and "witchy" feeling of creating your potion.

If you are making an infusion of herbs in hot water, be careful not to boil the water, as this can break down beneficial compounds in the herbs.

Here is a sample potion, intended to induce calm alertness:

## *Sample: A Potion to Induce Calm Alertness*

This potion is intended to induce calm alertness.

**You will need**

Moon water (2 cups or 475 ml)

Coffee filter

Dried spearmint

Dried chamomile

Dried hyssop

Dried rose petals

Dried melissa (lemon balm)

Tea ball or sachet

Pen and paper

Beaker or mug

PROCESS

First make moon water by sitting two cups of water out in the light of the full Moon overnight. The next morning, clean the water with a coffee filter to remove impurities. Then bring to a full boil, and cool to room temperature.

Take the two cups (475 ml) of cooled Moon water and add to it one large pinch dried spearmint, one large pinch dried chamomile, a pinch of dried hyssop, a pinch of dried rose petals and one of melissa (lemonbalm) in a tea ball or sachet.

Create a sigil (see page 84) using the words *alert* and *calm*. Inscribe your sigil on a small piece of plain white paper with a pencil.

Bring the Moon water mixture to 180° F. (82° C), and pour into a beaker or large mug.

Insert the sachet, saying, "Steady, steady, steady, eyes sharp as falcons, may those that drink this be aware and calm."

Stir until the water is a rich, golden-green color.

Float the sigil atop the beaker in which you are infusing your potion. Wait for it to soak and sink. Then say, "Eyes sharp as falcons, heart steady, without worry," and sip the potion slowly.

Now, you are probably aware that you have just brewed yourself a cup of herbal tea. But isn't this a much more wonderful and compelling way to do that? And calm and alertness are sure to follow. Don't underestimate that placebo effect.

## Written Intentions

When you think about it, writing is a spell: an arbitrary written symbol summons a sound to your mind, and in combinations, entire complex meanings. So writing down our intentions or situations "captures" them, in a way, enabling us to do physical things with them.

I find that writing my intentions, hopes, fears or challenges on a small piece of paper or a dried leaf and then folding it or sealing it with sealing or candle wax to "trap" it within the paper gives me many ritual options for dealing with the life circumstance or aspiration written on it. I can burn the paper in a cauldron or a small dish to dispel the contents; I can bury it either to be done with it and let it go back to the Earth, or as a "seed" from which will sprout my desires. I can cast it into water where it will dissolve and disappear. Some cultures hang symbols of their wishes in trees—you can do that with your written wishes as well.

In my household at the winter solstice every year, we burn a Midwinter log made from the trunk of the previous year's Midwinter tree, decorated with green boughs, pinecones, holly and mistletoe and into which we tuck little notes with our hopes for the coming year (see page 177 for directions for making a Midwinter log). When we burn the log, we send these hopes "out into the world," where we hope they will be born. This is just one example of the kind of rituals you can do with written language—another, *sigils,* is discussed on page 84.

## Cauldron Rituals

The cauldron is a stereotypical piece of "witchy equipment," featured in depictions of magic-making from Shakespeare to political cartoons. Generally made of cast iron, a cauldron can serve many ritual functions: as a receiver for ingredients in a ritual potion, as a container in which to burn things like papers, sigils, or incense, or as a vessel for simmering soups or hot drinks (so long as you haven't used toxic ingredients in the cauldron *ever*). It can be used as a symbolic container, or a wishing well. Be creative! There is nothing quite so charming, homey, evocative of olden times and magic as the sight of a cauldron in the hearth, on a fire, or nestled in coals.

If your cauldron has a lid, you can warm herbs or a couple of drops of essential oil on top of the closed lid to create pleasant and evocative scents in your home or fire pit area.

While the traditional three-legged, pot-bellied cast-iron cauldron is attractive and atmospheric, they can be expensive, so my cauldron is an old, slightly rusty Dutch oven, which conveys an air of antiquity and charm. You can often find them at flea markets and second-hand stores.

## Divination

Let me say at the outset: insofar as all evidence suggests, fortune-telling isn't real. We can't see the future. There are a variety of physical theories as to why this should be so.

We can, however, learn a lot more about the present than we know now. And particularly, we can learn about what is going on in our subconscious minds by working with symbols and developing narratives from them. This is "spicy psychology" at its best, and why divination practices are useful.

Divination systems like reading Tarot cards or oracle cards present rich sets of symbols from which to choose. When we turn over and read the cards, even though the cards are randomly ordered, the meanings we select from this abundance of symbols can tell us truths we have been avoiding and give us new insights into the situations of our lives.

Other systems, like finding symbols in tea leaves or patterns in the configurations of bones thrown or shapes in wax dripped in water or clouds or … anything, really … similarly give us a way of noting what kinds of symbols our brains are choosing to identify. This can tell us about ourselves and our current states.

Divination can be an insightful and useful "subconscious diagnostic" tool. Besides, it can be fun! Light some candles and get out the cards or the bones and you will find you are almost instantly in the ritual state of focus and presence. There are few things more conducive to the witchy, "magical" atmosphere than divination practices.

## Scented Oils

You can make "oil potions" that will carry the scents of herbs you have added to a base of a neutral-smelling oil like grapeseed or canola. You can use these as body scents or to anoint tools or materials you use in rituals. If you are going to apply them to your body, make sure you don't have any sensitivities to the herbs in question. Be aware that unless they are kept cold, these oils will eventually go rancid, so use them promptly.

## Sigils

Over the centuries, many cultures have used drawn symbols to communicate ritual meaning. Examples ranging from Roman curse scrolls incised on lead sheets to European ceremonial magic in Enochian script to Vodoun *vé-vés* have signified the invocation of results, magical beings or deities. This is an old practice, and one you can use as well.

A *sigil,* or magical symbol, is a sort of "shorthand" for a ritual intention: a "barcode for the brain," if you will, that invokes a particular meaning for you when you see it. As such, it can be a powerful way of reminding yourself of your intention and reinforcing its power.

This is not arbitrary, or trivial. We acknowledge symbols as having deep meaning all the time, from flags to stop signs to biohazard symbols. Our minds are capable of seizing on symbols far more rapidly than linear strings of text: they touch us at deeper levels than written language ever can.

So let's make some! There are many ways to make ritual sigils, so don't feel limited by this, but here is one way to create your own:

### *Center Yourself*

Sit quietly and take some deep breaths. Concentrate on your breathing until you feel you are calm, relaxed, and present. To facilitate this, you may want to create an appropriate setting with some magical tools, symbols, and possibly by working by candlelight.

### *Identify Your Intention*

This is an affirmative statement of your intention for creating the sigil, stated as a fact, such as "I am courageous" or "I have abundance in my life" or "I am healthy in mind and body." Take time to craft a statement that exactly expresses your desired outcome for this ritual work.

Try something that really challenges your biases and preconceived beliefs about yourself and your life. If you believe you are weak, state that you are strong. If you believe you aren't good enough, state that you are better than good enough. Avoid using negatives in the sentence, as your subconscious can easily edit out the "not" and turn your sentence from "I am not weak" to "I am ... weak!"

- **Write out the sentence.** Use capital letters, in print... or if you like your sigils baroque, use cursive.

- **Cross out the vowels and scramble the letters.** Alternatively, some people cross out every other letter and then scramble the letters.
- Now comes the creative part: on a square of paper, **draw a symbol that combines the letters in some way.** You can distort, augment, remove parts of and/or add to the letters until the symbol looks "right" to you, and add shapes to it as you wish. In drawing your final version, you can use pencil, pen, charcoal, ink and brush and/or special paper to make your sigil more special and magical seeming.

Now you have your magical sigil. The next step is to ritually "activate" it to build the association between the symbol and its meaning in your mind.

Conduct a ritual in which you "charge" the sigil with Qualities you wish for it to conduct. Start by creating a contemplative, sacred space: perhaps by candlelight, with some incense burning and music playing that takes you into the ritual state. You might sprinkle it with salt water to invoke the cyclical nature of the ocean's tides, or drip dots of colored wax from a candle of a particular color.

Next—and this is important—say the sigil's meaning over it, slowly and clearly and repeatedly. Perhaps thirteen times, one for each cycle of the Moon in a year, or any other number that has significance for you. When you are done chanting the meaning sentence over the sigil, fold each of the paper's four corners inward until they all touch, and seal the paper shut with a dot of sealing wax, "locking the magic in" and the secret meaning of your sigil.

Place the sealed sigil on your Focus. Draw another copy of it on a piece of paper so there is a visible version on your Focus as well.

Now, post your sigil where you can see it! On your dressing mirror, inside a cabinet in your kitchen that you open every morning, on your car dashboard, etc. Every time you see it is like repeating your intention statement to yourself, reinforcing your belief in its validity; in fact, because it is a graphic illustration rather than a linear string of characters, the sigil touches the deeper, metaphorical part of your mind. You will find that over time, your ability to instantly recognize and "read" a sigil—just as you do a letter of the alphabet—will become refined and automatic.

Over time, a sigil may become "stale"—you overlook it because you have seen it so many times that it no longer becomes a subject of focus. If this happens, unseal the sigil from your Focus, and recharge the sigil. This will remind you of the seriousness of the intention you put behind creating it, and why its meaning is so important to you.

## Talismans

Remember that lucky athlete's jersey I mentioned earlier? It's an example of a very old ritual technique called a talisman.

A *talisman* is a "magic object": an object imbued with associations through a ritual and then carried to remind the carrier of the ritual's meaning and experience. Commonly carried talismans include stones, coins, and other small items, but such items as a "lucky" piece of clothing could be considered talismanic.

A ritual to create a talisman can be as elaborate or as simple as you like, but the more vivid the memory of creating the talisman, the more influential it is likely to be on your confidence and mental state.

## But Wait, There's More!

These are some of the ritual arts that are commonly used by ritual practitioners to influence their minds, express their creativity, and create psychological change. But there are many more! Use your imagination to create your own.

Details on how to do many of these ritual arts are in the resource section at the back of the book.

# Part 2
# Rituals in Practice

# Chapter 7
# Occasions for Celebrating Rituals

Now that you know how to create a ritual, when is a good time to do one?

Well, there are multiple answers to this question. Generally, occasions for rituals fall into three broad categories: *cyclic celebrations, rites of passage,* and *personal rituals.* These serve different purposes, and in your personal practice you may find yourself more drawn to one kind of ritual than the others. That's fine! Your practice is for you.

We will explore each of these types of rituals in turn, with simple sample rituals for each occasion.

## Cyclical Celebrations

Cyclical celebrations mark the passage of time in cycles: the coming of spring, for example, or the longest night of the year, or a particular phase of the Moon. The most commonly celebrated cyclical ritual celebrations observe the solar cycle, or the passage of the seasons of the year. This is known in Pagan circles as the *Wheel of the Year.*

One approach to developing a celebratory personal spiritual practice around the course of the year is to celebrate the eight holidays (or *sabbaths)* of the Pagan "Wheel of the Year." These holidays are natural for people to observe because they are grounded in real events rather than mythological ones: the solar solstices and equinoxes, and the midpoints between them. The solstices are the longest and shortest days of the year; the equinoxes are the points at which the day is roughly equal in length with the night.

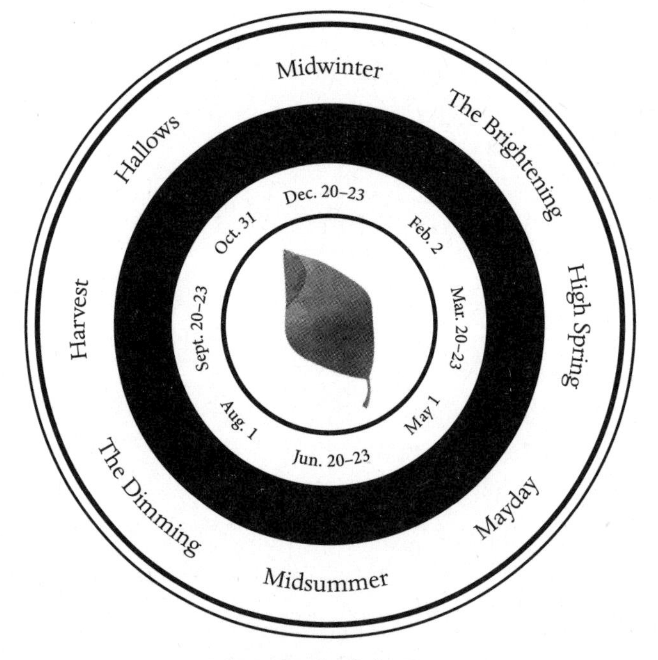


***The Wheel of the Year***

For those in the Northern Hemisphere, here are the holidays of the Wheel of the Year. There are many names for these holidays—I prefer those used here because they are not rooted in any particular culture and can thus been seen as somewhat universal:

- **Midwinter** or **Yule:** the winter solstice: celebrated on or around December 21.
- **The Brightening:** the midpoint between Midwinter and the spring equinox, celebrated in the first week of February.
- **High Spring** or the vernal or spring equinox: celebrated on or about the 20st of March.

- **May Day** (or **Summertide** in the Southern Hemisphere): the midpoint between High Spring and the summer solstice, celebrated in the first week of May.
- **Midsummer:** The summer solstice, celebrated on or around June 20.
- **The Dimming:** the midpoint between Midsummer and the autumnal equinox, celebrated in the first week of August. Sometimes also known as "Summer's Waning."
- **Harvest** or the autumnal equinox: celebrated on or around the 20th of September.
- **Hallows:** the midpoint between Harvest and Midwinter, celebrated October 31 into the first week of November.

### *For Readers in the Southern Hemisphere*

Because the solar cycles of the two hemispheres are reversed, the seasonal holidays described herein are flipped by six months for the Southern Hemisphere calendar. Midwinter, therefore, is around June 20, the Brightening at the beginning of August, etc.

You can celebrate these holidays just as well as folks in the north and rename them as seems appropriate to you! It may feel a little weird at first to celebrate Midwinter in June, but that's because the mainstream culture persists with holding their winter holiday, Christmas, at the height of the summer in your area. Disregard this—your practice is yours and you can implement it as you like.

### *Marking Time*

The point of cyclical celebrations is to pay attention to the passing of time. It is so easy for our lives simply to fly by, but a ritual practice helps us to slow down, to mark the comings and goings of the seasons and what they mean for us, both practically and metaphorically.

Accordingly, there are habits to be cultivated if we are to truly know what is going on in the natural world around us. Most importantly, we must simply slow down and take notice of the changes in the world as they happen. We must take time to smell flowers, admire birds and animals, notice the life stages of trees and plants, be aware of the phases of the Moon and the slow turning of the sky through the seasons.

A great way to get into this habit is by keeping a *phenology journal.* A phenology journal is a record, usually filled out every day, or at least every week, in which you simply record what you see as you sit somewhere or go on a short walk. What is the weather like? What's the temperature? What are the plants and trees doing? Do you see birds or animals—what did they look like?

Over time, a phenology journal will provide you with a data set about what your particular area's natural cycles are like. This can help you to adjust the generalized descriptions of seasonal celebrations from this book to specifically address your own natural environment.

In some cases, this may mean completely reworking your Wheel of the Year from what I describe here. If you live in subtropical or tropical climes, or far northern or southern areas, you may find that the cycle of the year I describe for temperate areas simply does not work for you at all, and you need to redefine the holidays to reflect your surroundings.

There is nothing wrong with that. It is absolutely the right thing to do to conform the described framework to your lived experience, rather than the reverse. It makes no sense to celebrate the coming of spring if it is twenty degrees outside and snowing!

Following, I will describe each of the eight sabbaths of the Wheel of the Year, with a little poem to introduce each, some history, and some themes and practices you may want to incorporate into your own seasonal celebrations. Feel free to adapt to your circumstances and wishes—this is your practice!

The instructions for craft projects and recipes listed under each sabbath can be found in the Resources section later in the book.

### A Quick Note on "Correspondences"

Many guides to celebrating the Wheel of the Year rely heavily on what are called *correspondences:* the association of particular colors, symbols, plants, stones, zodiacal signs, etc., with a given holiday.

While I provide some associative themes for each of the eight holidays of the Wheel of the Year, it is important to remember that all such correspondences are arbitrary: there is nothing inherent about blue, or quartz, or holly plants, to give a few examples, that necessarily associates them with a particular season or day in the year. Anyone telling you otherwise is simply blowing smoke.

What is most important is what you associate with these things. If black and orange are winter solstice colors to you, by all means use them in your Midwinter decorating. And if something listed here feels "off" to you, feel free to ignore it! The important point is that you are crafting a spiritual calendar for yourself and your fellow celebrants. It has to work for you.

## Midwinter

*Whilst outside the cold wind howls*
*Within burns the hearth fire*
*Keeping hope alive for spring*

Midwinter, the shortest day (and longest night) of the year on December 20 or 21 (June 20 or 21 in the Southern Hemisphere), marks the season of celebration before the hardship of winter truly sets in. Historically, in temperate areas this was the time that the last perishable foods gathered in the harvest were consumed before they decayed, and so feasts and parties were traditional.

Cultures all over the world have ways of celebrating the winter solstice, and the accumulation of many of those traditions lives with us today in the form of Christmas, Chanukah, the Pagan Yule, Krampusnacht, and newer traditions such as Kwanzaa and even Festivus, the humorous holiday "for the rest of us" created by the television sitcom *Seinfeld*. Themes often include the "birth" of the Sun, which begins its long swing back to the lengthy days of summer at this point in the year. Symbolically represented with candles and lights in the darkness, we know that Midwinter has been celebrated for thousands of years because of stone observatories that line up exactly with the winter solstice sunrise, such as Ireland's Newgrange, England's Stonehenge, and other such prehistoric constructions throughout the world.

For atheists and other non-believers who don't subscribe to traditional religious practices at this time of year, navigating this season today in a manner free of theistic and supernatural overtones can be a bit of a challenge. We're besieged with well-intentioned messages from relatives and friends rooted in their religious beliefs. Exasperating as it can sometimes be, the main thing is to remember that more often than not, those expressions are meant kindly and with love, not to try to shove religious credulity down our throats.

Christmas, of course, is a big deal in mainstream Western culture, and so is Midwinter for my community, as the beginning of the new year's cycle and the moment the Sun begins to reemerge from the deepest of winter's depths. Many cultures associate evergreen plants and trees with this season, as they remain active and green during the cold months, and so we erect a Midwinter tree similar to a Christmas tree. Our Midwinter tree is surmounted by a Sun, and our ornaments are mostly of natural creatures and symbols: a moon, a salmon, a bat, an owl, mushrooms, apples, trees—even an octopus!—as well as the Atheopagan Suntree symbol (see page 19). We also have a small collection of very old Christmas ornaments from the 1940s and 1950s, which remind us of the ornaments our parents had during our childhoods, memories of which are always so present at this time of year.

On Midwinter night, one of my community's traditions has been to make ourselves hot cider or mulled wine (see the recipe for this holiday), turn off all lights in the house and go to sit outside in silence, contemplating the cold and darkness, reminding ourselves of the blessings we enjoy that keep us warm and loved and fed and safe at this bitter time of year. After a half-hour or so, we return indoors, sing songs, light candles to "bring the newborn light back" into the home, and burn our Midwinter log in an annual ritual of hope and inspiration (see the craft resources at the end of the book).

Then we drink a toast and dig into a rich dinner, sing some more songs and enjoy one another's company. For surely we can't have Midwinter without music! Here are a couple of re-written Christmas classics I have re-written with secular lyrics—one silly, one serious:

**AXIAL TILT (TUNE: SILENT NIGHT)**

Axial tilt
The way the world's built:
Sun is north, then sun is south.
Axial precession makes seasons occur;
Sometimes bikinis and other times fur.
Insert metaphor here!
Insert metaphor here.

Evergreen tree
Holly berry
Things that stay alive, you see.
Meanwhile freezing and darkness reign
We'd much rather have fun than complain.
We are still alive!
We are still alive.

We're so hoping
Soon will come Spring
Meanwhile let's eat, drink, and sing!
Friends and relations convene by the fire
Cold and darkness don't seem quite so dire.
Pass the gravy please!
Pass the gravy please.
*(repeat first verse)*

**OH DARKEST NIGHT (TUNE: O HOLY NIGHT)**

Oh darkest night, the stars are brightly shining
It is the night of the dawning new year.
Here in the dark, for sun and warmth we're pining

But we are cheered by our friends and family here.
The cold bright stars: a trillion worlds above us
As here on Earth we gather loved ones near.
Raise up your eyes, and see the Cosmos' wonder
Oh Night sublime
Oh night, oh darkest night
Oh Night sublime
Oh night, oh night sublime.

**Themes:** Gestation and birth, family, community, new beginnings and hopes, light, persistence, the Sun

**Thematic décor colors and symbols:** Green, gold, red, evergreen plants

**Ritual activities:** Lighted and decorated Midwinter tree, household decoration with colorful lighting, vigil in darkness

**Craft projects:** Midwinter log ritual

**Recipes:** Mulled wine

## The Brightening

*At last the days lengthen*
*Cozy in our beds*
*We can at least dream of spring*

The Brightening, at the beginning of February for those in the northern hemisphere or beginning of August in the south, is the midpoint between the winter solstice and the vernal, or spring equinox.

By this point in the year, the deep darkness of winter has receded. Days are noticeably longer, but the cold and fierce weather of winter are still very much present in most areas.

This is a time when those prone to depression can really struggle. The festivities of Midwinter have long since passed, and the days are cold, still short and dim, with quite a bit more of that to look forward to before spring arrives.

It is therefore a really good idea to have a holiday at this time! It's an excuse for gathering with loved ones, dreaming up visions and plans for what we seek to make real in the coming year cycle, and celebrating the small ones among us at "their time of year."

Where I live, this is the rainiest time of the year, and so I celebrate water and its many blessings, calling the local holiday "Riverain." This is an example of how you might adapt your own Wheel of the Year to reflect the conditions in your local area.

In the agricultural cycle of the year for temperate areas, it is typically still too cold and the days are too short to start planting yet, but this is when planning for a garden or farm should take place, and tools should be sharpened and refurbished. Some cultures associate this time of year with the forge, anvil and hammer for this reason; you can incorporate these symbols into your rituals if you wish. Food stores were also often running low by this point; the recipe provided for this holiday, for soda bread, requires only dry ingredients which can persist in storage until this time of year.

Ritually, too, themes of dreams, wishes and plans can be good at this time of year. A "wishing well" can be created from a decorated bowl or a cauldron, and during the Brightening ritual's Working phase, participants can cast an object (traditionally a coin) into the well while making a wish for the near future. Bury the objects so the wishes will "grow" with the swelling year.

The craft projects provided for this holiday include making incense, laying in a good stock of which is always helpful to be prepared for rituals around the year, and directions for making a dream sachet filled with dried mugwort, which is traditionally said to facilitate vivid and meaningful dreams when placed under the pillow.

**Themes:** Infancy, Dreaming/Planning, Preparation of tools

**Thematic décor colors and symbols:** Blue, white, gold; cradle and baby; forge, anvil and hammer, water well

**Ritual activities:** Wishing well, Year's cradle

**Craft project (s):** Incense, dream sachet

**Recipe:** Soda bread, Borsch Root Soup

## High Spring

*Flowers laugh across meadows*
*As here on the equal day and night*
*We celebrate children, both in and out*

High Spring, at the vernal or spring equinox on or about March 20 (September 20 in the Southern Hemisphere), is one of two points in the year when the day and the night throughout the world are roughly the same length, because the equator is in line with the plane of the Earth's orbit around the Sun (called the Ecliptic). This holiday is a time to celebrate children of up to pre-teen age and to get in touch with our own childlike innocence.

Now, depending on the climate where you live, this can be the beginning of spring or a time still marked by snow and cold weather. At higher latitudes and elevations, the advent of spring can be significantly delayed. But in many places, the end of March is a time of sprouting new growth, even if it is just green shoots above the surface of the snow and buds on the trees. In areas where it is warmer, it is the time for planting gardens and starting to implement those plans we were dreaming up at the Brightening.

Historically, this time of year was associated in Europe with eggs, because birds were laying and chickens (which are influenced by the amount of daylight in their laying schedules) had begun to lay more frequently again. It is also a time when sheep are bearing lambs, so chicken, egg and lamb imagery are common in traditional European crafts associated with this time of year.

My community likes to celebrate this holiday with childlike activities like dying colored eggs and playing children's games like hopscotch, Chutes and Ladders and CandyLand. It's a great time to cut loose, be silly and childlike and enjoy being with children. It is a day when we pay special attention to kids and let them take a lead role in our celebratory ritual:

after the egg dying is done, for example, children can take baskets of them around the circle of celebrants, distributing them to each person (helps to have your own basket to receive them!) as a special blessing of the season.

Another common ritual element is the planting of seeds, which can be nurtured and grow as the seasons progress. I like to use sunflower seeds, which can be transplanted into the ground when large enough, to grow tall and dramatic at the holiday of The Dimming.

This is an activity we can also do as the Working in a circle, distributing little pots filled with potting soil and seeds that each celebrant can plant. Then the group can sing a song or chant to bless the seeds with our hopes and wishes for the coming season's harvest.

Finally, there is enough sunlight at this point in the year that it is traditional to do some spring cleaning: organizing, de-cluttering, getting rid of the old in order to make room for the new. There is nothing like the good feeling attained when a good thorough cleansing of your space has been achieved.

**Themes:** childhood, planting of seeds for the coming harvest

**Thematic décor colors and symbols:** sky blue, pink and purple; dyed/painted eggs, rabbits, birds

**Craft project:** Natural egg dyeing

**Recipe:** Raspberry lemonade

## May Day

*Dance the Maypole round about!*
*Flirt and sing and shout!*
*Sumer is a-comin' in and winter's gone away!*

May Day (on or around the first of May in the Northern Hemisphere, or November 1 in the Southern) in England is traditionally a time to celebrate the beginning of summer. Gardens are being tended now and some of the days, in most places at least, are warm and dry. Wildflowers are prolific in many areas.

Historically, "going a-Maying" was an activity for young adults: going into the forests to pick flowers and enjoy some alone time without supervision of parents. So we associate May Day not only with young adulthood, but with sexuality and the pleasures of nature.

The most famous ritual associated with May Day, of course, is the Maypole: a tall pole festooned with flowers and ribbons, about which celebrants dance, weaving the ribbons into a colorful pattern on the pole. This is a joyous ritual and many centuries old: in fact, the sourpuss conservative English dictator Oliver Cromwell banned Maypoles (as well as festivities celebrating Christmas) in the seventeenth century.[8]

Fortunately, that didn't last, and we are able to enjoy both today. In the Crafts Projects resource section at the end of the book you will find all you need to know about how to erect and dance with a Maypole.

May Day is also known internationally as a time to celebrate workers and labor, so be sure to appreciate the working people who make your life better—not just at this time of year, but all year round.

There are many folk traditions associated with May Day. In its association with young adulthood, one such tradition was that dew collected on the morning of May Day and used to wash the face would preserve beauty and a young appearance. Another tradition was to gather posies (small bouquets) of flowers and leave them on the doorsteps of neighbors or loved ones. If you research a bit, you can find all sorts of May traditions.

For adults, of course, this being the holiday that celebrates sexuality, you can devise private rituals of your own if you wish, to taste! In the seasonal crafts appendix, I include a flirty, consent-based May Day game called the Consensual Pomander Ball.

**Themes:** Young adulthood, sexuality, fertility, responsibility, consent, summer's arrival

**Thematic décor colors:** Green and gold

**Ritual elements:** Maypole ritual

8. Lincoln, Margarette, *London and the Seventeenth Century: The Making of the World's Greatest City* (Yale University Press), 2022

**Craft Projects:** Flower Crown, Maypole, Consensual Pomander Ball (game)

**Recipe:** May wine, Strawberry Sage Shrub

## Midsummer

*Ahh the long evenings, warm and sweet*
*A time for friends and feasting*
*Soon comes the work of the harvests*

The summer solstice, on or around June 20 (December 20 in the Southern Hemisphere), is the longest day of the year, and the shortest night. It's no surprise that right around that time are celebrations throughout the Northern Hemisphere involving outdoor barbecues, trips to lakes and beaches, and camping.

The long evenings at this time of year—often combined with warm but not excessive temperatures—make for lovely times to hang out with friends and family, and our Midsummer celebrations are no exception.

In the traditional agricultural cycle of Europe, this was also a time of leisure. The planting was done and the crops weren't yet ripe for harvesting. Time to tap a barrel of last year's beer and enjoy life.

As we view a human life's arc along the Wheel of the Year, Midsummer is full adulthood: the adult at the height of their powers, working hard to build a family, a career or whatever else motivates them. A time to recognize all the effort that goes into such enterprises and raise a toast, perhaps, to the thirty- and forty-somethings in your circle of friends.

It's a time for getting outdoors, and I like to do my Midsummer celebration at a park or at a beach, where people can relax, celebrate, and have a good time. As the day finally wanes, light a fire to carry the solar feeling into the night, and make some music!

Sometimes that's all the ritual I need for a Midsummer: just people I care about, enjoying themselves. But I do have other ritual activities I carry out for Midsummer, such as refreshing my Sun broom (see the seasonal crafts appendix on page 177), which is a ritual tool I use during the dark months to evoke a sense of sunshine and warmth.

The long days, like everything in life, do not last, so seize them! Make plans to gather and celebrate this comfortable, beautiful time of year.

**Themes:** leisure, enjoyment; a break from hard work and effort; responsibility

**Thematic décor colors and symbols:** Sun symbols, gold, yellow, blue

**Ritual elements:** hammocks!

**Craft project:** Sun broom

**Recipe:** Mojitos

## The Dimming

*We can see it now*
*The year draws down*
*First harvest is here*

The Dimming is the midpoint between Midsummer and the autumnal equinox, falling in the first week in August (or February, in the Southern Hemisphere). Traditionally, this is the time of the first harvest: that of grains and other early crops such as alfalfa. As a result, the Catholic holiday around this time was named "Lammas" (Anglo-Saxon *hlaf-mas* or Loaf-Mass), and it is associated with bread, beer, and all things grain-related.

By this point in the year, the days have noticeably shortened from their peak at Midsummer. Autumn is on the way, and some of the early signs may already be evident: a change in the blue tint of the sky, a notable change to the angle of the Sun, and often, the hottest weather of the year.

Where I live, the leaves of the oaks and buckeyes and bay laurel have darkened now from their bright new spring colors. Fog rolls in from the ocean every evening, then burns off the next morning, leaving sparkling and temperate days punctuated by the occasional scorcher. Birds are fattening up before they migrate, clustering around our feeders and in the nearby trees. It is the time of preparation for the impending grape harvest, known locally as The Crush, which is the main harvesting event of our local agriculture.

The Dimming is a time to reflect on the early gifts this year cycle has brought us: our own personal first harvests. As the year is measured in relation to a human life, it is the time of middle age, and we celebrate those at the height of their careers and power at this time, and the fruits of those powers may be celebrated now as well: technology, engineering, scientific discovery. Children may now be grown and leaving home for school or work; long-sought advancements may have been achieved. It is the time to express gratitude for these developments and celebration that our lives have led us to this place.

Historically, this was the time of athletic contests such as the Olympic Games and outdoor play may be a part of your celebrations, like a rousing game of volleyball or tug-of-war. If you want to be traditional like the Ancient Greeks, do them naked!

**Themes:** First (or early) harvest, middle age, products of long efforts such as technology and scientific discovery

**Thematic décor colors and symbols:** brown and gold, grain sheaves and loaves of bread, harvest tools such as sickles

**Ritual activities:** singing *John Barleycorn Must Die*, group sports

**Craft project:** Ritual Mask

**Recipe:** Rye bread

## Harvest

*Riches pour from the good Earth.*
*The work is done.*
*Let us enjoy!*

The autumnal equinox, on or about September 20 (March 20 in the Southern Hemisphere), is the second point in the year when days and nights are of equal length. Days may still be warm, but crisp nights often follow. Autumn has arrived.

Where I live, this is the height of The Crush, the harvest and crushing of grapes to begin the process of fermenting wine. Gardens are pouring out vegetables and my region's status as an agricultural producer is apparent in the many fruit stands, roadside vendors, and the fresh local produce available in stores.

We name this holiday *Harvest*, not only because it is the time of agricultural gathering-in, but also to note this stage in a human life: the time of receiving and assessment of what one's plans have achieved, of fulfillment of long effort. It is a time when we celebrate the elderly among us with gratitude for their wisdom and their accomplishments.

Centering as it does on gratitude, abundance and achievement, feasts to celebrate Harvest featuring local agricultural products (where possible) are a common way to celebrate. There is nothing like a table groaning with food and drink surrounded by lively loved ones to instill a sense of well-being: that life is good. Of course, like all the sabbaths, the holiday can be celebrated solo or as a family, as well.

Our ritual at such a feast centers on expressing appreciation: to the Earth and Sun which brought forth the food and sustain us, to the many people involved in growing, harvesting, transporting, and preparing food for our table. Gratitude is such an important element of a well-lived life, and this holiday places it front-and-center for our recognition and embrace.

**Themes:** Gratitude, abundance, achievement, elderhood

**Thematic décor colors and symbols:** Rust, gold, brown, purple; the cornucopia

**Ritual activities:** feasting, gratitude circle

**Craft projects:** Corn Dolly

**Recipes:** Autumn Harvest Salad, Red Vegetable Curry

## Hallows

*Ancestors and bygone loved ones*
*Are remembered now:*
*Memento mori*

In the traditional agricultural cycle of the year, Hallows is the third harvest: the harvest of flesh. At this time, livestock herds were thinned down to what could be fed over the winter, and meat was dried, salted and smoked to preserve it for winter food. And so it is natural, as the days shorten, the cold draws in and the leaves drop from the trees, to associate this time with death and decomposition.

The midpoint between Harvest and Midwinter typically falls around the 6 or 7 of November (or around the 6 of May in the Southern Hemisphere), so the first weekend of November is when I celebrate it with my ritual circle, Dark Sun. Hallows traditions are many, of course, and mostly focused on Halloween, the 31st of October. It is a time when we remember our mortality, and scare ourselves with mock blood, reminders of death and tales of unnatural monsters returned from the dead. So if you wish—as I do!—you can celebrate Hallows for a full week, from Halloween to the actual date of Hallows.

My ritual circle, Dark Sun, has been together for more than thirty years now, and Hallows has always been a high point in our year, when we follow a similar ritual each time and do an overnight gathering so we can enjoy one another's company. Our members are somewhat far-flung geographically, so this isn't possible very often.

Our ritual is held every year at the home of Dark Sun members who live surrounded by forested land. It begins by gathering after dark around a Focus of seasonal symbols—a glowing jack o' lantern, bones, skulls, pictures of ancestors and departed loved ones, ritual tools—in a circle with a fire laid in the fire pit, but unlit.

We close our eyes and ground ourselves to attain the trance state and invoke the Qualities we hope will be with us as we go through this year's sabbath ritual. We prepare ourselves for the journey that is to come. We say all the Last Things we need to say before we go.

And then we turn our back on life, and walk off into the darkness in silence, to a dark area of the woods we have designated the Land of the Dead.

When we arrive there, we speak to those who have died in the previous year. We speak of our feelings about their deaths, we wish them well, we say whatever we need to say. It is a serious and emotional ritual in which we seek and find a feeling of connection with those who have left us.

And when it is done, when cold is seeping into our bones and the Land of the Dead is starting to feel a little too comfortable, we make our way back, light the fire, sing and pass wine and chocolate, and celebrate being alive.

It's a simple ritual, but a powerful one. And with each year, the depth of its power grows as we realize how many times we have done it, how many times we have passed this season together, knowing that one day, there will be first one gap in the circle, then another, and another, as our lives end.

Note that the "voyage to the Land of the Dead" could be done as a guided meditation rather than a literal traipse through the woods, for those who don't have access to such a place. In this case, you can do a guided meditation in which participants literally row across the river Styx to the Land of the Dead.

This is also the time of year that I update my Death Packet: a collection of papers including my will, medical directives, wishes for disposal of my body, social media passwords, life insurance information, farewell letter to those who survive me, funeral wishes, and so forth. Having this packet completed and in a place known to my loved ones is a gift I can offer them, so they don't have to scramble for information while grieving.[9]

9. You can download a blank workbook that will help you to create your own Death Packet at https://atheopaganism.org/wp-content/uploads/2018/10/death-and-dying-workbook-blank1.docx

Other traditions for the Hallows season include cooking family recipes and setting out food and drink—or pouring out libations of wine or other favorite drink on the ground—for the beloved dead. One very old tradition is a Silent Supper, held in complete silence to commune with the dead, and at which a place is set for the dead, with the very best of each dish served to them. The plate can be placed outside to be "taken by the dead" (or local wildlife) after the meal. Don't make a habit of this—feeding wildlife teaches them to depend on humans and is bad for them—but once a year shouldn't be a problem.

So have both, this Hallows season: the creepy fun of Halloween, and the solemn reflection on those we have lost and on your own mortality. You will find that, over time, both your grief and your natural fear of death become less acute, more manageable.

**Themes:** Death, decay

**Thematic décor colors and symbols:** black, orange, blood red, skulls and bones, the scythe of Death, hourglasses, pictures of ancestors and departed loved ones

**Ritual activities:** Ancestor veneration, contemplation of mortality, third-harvest feasting, pouring of libations / making offerings to the dead, death planning.

**Craft projects:** Carving jack o'lanterns; Fireball effect for rituals

**Recipes:** Barmbrack, Funeral Raisin Pie

## Other Occasions for Celebrating Rituals

The solar holidays, of course, aren't the only opportunities for cyclical rituals in your life. Before we talk about rites of passage, let's look at some more possibilities.

### *Celebrating the Cycles of the Moon*

Many Pagans like to observe the night of the full Moon (or, in some cases, other phases such as the new Moon) as a special monthly occurrence. It's a perfect time for moonlit walks and setting intentions for the coming month: by the next full Moon, what will you have done?

Some see the new Moon as a time for launching new projects with the goal of attaining them by the full Moon, and perhaps integrating them during the waning phases.

A monthly Moon practice can add a layer of specialness to the passage of the months in addition to your celebration of the solar holidays.

Some Atheopagans associate the thirteen annual cycles of the Moon with the 13 Atheopagan Principles; so, the first Full Moon is the Skeptic's Moon, second is the Reverence Moon, etc., on through the thirteen Moon cycle of the year, in December, as follows:

- **First full Moon:** Skeptic's Moon
- **Second full Moon:** Reverence Moon
- **Third full Moon:** Gratitude Moon
- **Fourth full Moon:** Humility Moon
- **Fifth full Moon:** Humorous Moon
- **Sixth full Moon:** Praxis Moon
- **Seventh full Moon:** Inclusive Moon
- **Eighth full Moon:** Legacy Moon
- **Ninth full Moon:** Responsibility Moon
- **Tenth full Moon:** Pleasure Moon
- **Eleventh full Moon:** Curiosity Moon
- **Twelfth full Moon:** Integrity Moon
- **Thirteenth full Moon:** Kindness Moon

Each of these monthly celebrations is an opportunity to contemplate the meaning of the pertinent Principle, and perhaps to take action, as, for example during the Responsibility Moon you can develop a new social responsibility practice like volunteering for a social services agency.

## *Miscellaneous Holidays*

Celebration is fun, and we can invent reasons to do it! Here are some jolly, secular holidays to throw into your calendar just because. They add festivity and a sense of playfulness, which we can all use more of.

**SLOGG:** Third Saturday in January. A holiday simply to break the monotony of cold, gray, wet days. Celebrated with mulled wine, silly hats, board games and jigsaw puzzles.

**Pi Day:** March 14 (3.14, get it?) A day to bake and eat pie! This is also Einstein's birthday, so it's a good time to celebrate science and discovery.

**Yuri's Night:** April 12. Commemorates the first entry of a human into space, on April 12, 1961, when Yuri Gagarin orbited the Earth. Yuri's Night is celebrated with special events as the "World Space Party" at museums and observatories all over the world. Even if you don't hold or go to such an event, go outside on Yuri's Night and look up!

**Tau Day:** June 28 (6.28). Tau is double pi, or the ratio of a circle's radius to its circumference, so this day celebrates *twice as much pie!*

**Int'l Talk Like a Pirate Day:** September 19. Just what it says on the label. Details at talklikeapirate.com. ARRRR!

**Sagan's Day:** Nov. 9. The beloved astrophysicist and science educator was born on this day in 1934. Sagan's Day is an opportunity to celebrate not only science, but teachers and education as well. Getting young people excited about their world is a high calling.

**Wolfenoot:** Nov. 23. Invented by a seven-year-old, Wolfenoot is "about celebrating our pack—human and animal—helping where we can, and making the world a better, kinder place." It celebrates dogs, involves dog treats and cake shaped like a Moon. More at wolfenoot.com.

**First Snow** or **First Rain** or **Arrival of the Monsoons:** (whenever they happen). An opportunity for a spontaneous celebration, there is something wonderful about precipitation after a long wait.

There are plenty of additional holidays which you can adopt as desired. Have fun!

Chapter 8

# Rites of Passage

A *rite of passage* is a ritual marking the transition from one stage in life to another. Rites of passage are helpful because they enable us to change our status both in our own minds and in the eyes of the community to the new life stage (such as, from single to married) and to have a joyous commemoration of the event.

Throughout the world, rites of passage are major events in a person's life. In many cultures, a person's privileges, status, and even name may change after undergoing a rite of passage.

The English-speaking world, however, is rather impoverished when it comes to rites of passage. Most of us have no formal rite marking the transition from youth to adulthood, for instance, which can be a very important change. As a result, many report wondering, "Am I grown up yet?" even into their thirties or forties.

This chapter will describe some of the more common rites of passage as celebrated by people throughout the world, providing examples you can adapt for your own usage. You can avail yourself of as many of them as you wish. You may be surprised at how powerful these rituals can be, how much they change how you look at yourself and your role in your community.

## Parenthood

Rites are held to congratulate a parent or parents about to have a child or about to adopt into their family, or to welcome the new member of the family.

### *Rites to Honor Parents*

This ritual should be held late in a pregnancy in case a misfortune occurs earlier on. In the case of an adoption, this ceremony should be adapted to welcome and bless the new family member.

#### PREPARATION

Decorate festively and play upbeat music as guests arrival. When the time comes for the ritual, have guests sit in a circle around the parent(s).

#### ARRIVAL

The parent(s) sit in the center of the circle of guests. Guests sing a welcoming song of the parent(s) choosing.

#### QUALITIES

Guests call out the qualities they hope the family will experience together.

#### INTENTION

The parent(s) express their wishes for the new family member and for their relationship with the new member.

#### WORKING

- **Gifts:** Guests give gifts to the new parent(s) (and/or, if an adoption, to the new family member).

- **Stories and Wisdom:** Guests are invited to provide illuminating stories from their own experiences of parenthood, to help the new family along. A rattle or other object may be passed from speaker to speaker to keep the focus on one speaker at a time.
- **Other:** If the parent(s) have a ribbon-bedecked broom from their handfasting (wedding), the parent(s) may tie a new ribbon onto it to signify the addition to their family.

#### GRATITUDE

Community members offer what they are grateful for about their relationship with the parent(s).

#### BENEDICTION

Officiant says: "May this family be strong and happy, and filled with love. And may the love of this community support them as they grow. May all of us go forth to live upon this good Earth in joy!"

### *Welcoming Ceremonies*

Welcoming ceremonies are for newly born infants, both to formally welcome them into the world and to present them to their loved ones and community. Because newborns are delicate and often fussy, these rituals should be short, pithy and impactful. Here is a sample ritual for Welcoming:

#### ARRIVAL

Officiant invites the attendees to take three deep breaths and blow them out, letting the stresses and concerns of the day flow away from them, to arrive in presence for witnessing of this important rite.

#### QUALITIES

Officiant invites attendees to call out, in random order, qualities that they hope will be with the new baby and their parents as they grow.

#### WORKING

When Qualities are complete, officiant says, "We welcome this new life to Earth, the sweet planet which produced and sustains us all. We will name this new child and will acquaint them with the miraculous place from which they came."

- **Naming:** Officiant asks, "By what name do you choose to call this child?" Parents answer. Officiant declares, "Let it be known that this child is (name), and may they be honored and loved."
- **Anointing:** From a prepared bottle, the officiant (who has washed their hands immediately prior to the ritual), takes a small amount of water (which was previously boiled and cooled so as to be sterile), and brushes the lips of the child. Officiant says, "We welcome (name) to the Water Planet, Earth, and to all that water symbolizes for us."
- **Daubing:** Then, from a small dish of soil, the officiant brushes a little soil onto the soles of the new child's feet. "We welcome (name) to the beautiful land of Planet Earth, in the hopes that you will know much of this beauty during your life."

#### GRATITUDE

Parents express gratitude for the good things in their lives, and thank attendees for coming.

#### BENEDICTION

When the parents are done, officiant states, "I present (name) to their community. May they be loved, and of good fortune, and walk an honorable path on the good green Earth and may all of us go forth in joy to live!"

## Initiation into Teen Years and Adulthood

Parents can choose to formally acknowledge their children as they enter the time when they begin to differentiate from their parents and establish their autonomy. Here are two different rites for these moments.

### *Initiation into Teen Years*

While this isn't a transition to full adulthood, it is a period during which certain important milestones are attained (the legal opportunity to learn to drive a car, for example), and encounter with adult issues first becomes necessary (e.g., drugs and alcohol, sexuality).

This ritual is to be conducted by a Gathering Circle: four or more adult and teenaged family and loved ones of the subject who will conduct the ritual. At this subject's discretion, this may be a group made up only of the subject's gender, or the ritual may be performed only with the subject's parents if they prefer.

A note on consent: Such a ritual should only be conducted if the young person in question wants it. The option may be offered, and then the young person should choose.

Here is a sample ritual for coming into young adulthood:

PREPARATION

- **Ritual bathing:** In advance of the ritual, the subject should cleanse themselves, perhaps with special soap provided by the Gathering Circle.
- **Fasting:** Unless there are health reasons why they should not, the subject should fast during the day leading up to the ritual, drinking only water.
- **Ritual clothing:** A new set of clothes picked out by the subject can be worn.

ARRIVAL

First, the Gathering Circle convenes. They invoke the safety and power of the "ritual container" defined by the circle of attendees and note that humans have done these rituals for hundreds of thousands, if not millions of years—since before we were even fully human. The strength of community and the power of history are evoked as the circle comes together. A heartbeat rhythm is begun on a drum; it continues throughout the ritual (drum may be passed from circle member to circle member as fatigue sets in).

QUALITIES

In turn, passing a rattle, each member of the Gathering Circle speaks into the circle a characteristic, emotion, or value they wish to be included in the nature of the ritual. Examples could include maturity, wisdom, kindness, patience, discernment, and respect.

WORKING

- **Welcome:** The subject is then invited to enter the ritual space and stand in the center of the circle. Each member of the Gathering Circle welcomes the subject in turn, by name. Once welcomed, the subject is invited to sit.
- **Passing of Wisdom:** In turn, passing a rattle, each member of the Gathering Circle tells a wisdom story from their life, charging the subject with the powers and burdens of young adulthood: honor, exploration, autonomy, capability, sound judgment, discretion, consent. Particularly, the teenaged members of the Gathering Circle should provide guidance on navigating the teen years.
- **Breaking the Fast** and conveyance of young adulthood: Circulate sweet snacks and water or sweet juice to all. A designated Gathering Circle member states: "with this sweet taste, we impart the blessings of young adulthood to you." (The heartbeat drumbeat, which has been carried out throughout the ritual, ceases.)
- The young adult's **Pledge:** New young adult makes their declaration to the community: pledging to uphold the values they have imparted.
- **The Lasting Mark:** New young adult casts a hand outline on a sheet (perhaps four inches by six inches) of gray canvas (meant to symbolize a Paleolithic cave wall) with sprayed ocher-water (diluted brick-red tempra paint). While prehistoric artists of cave art sprayed their ocher paint by mouth,[10] you can use a spray bottle.

10. Lewis-Williams, David, *The Mind in the Cave* (London, Thames & Hudson), 2002

After the ritual and when dry, this canvas is rolled up and saved to be used for more such initiations by the same family or community going forward. Over time, it accumulates hand outlines of more young people moving toward adulthood—in the case of a community, perhaps many more. The first time this "imitation cave wall" is used, the members of the Gathering Circle may wish also to place their hand outlines on it, to establish the lineage of adults in the community.

If you are doing this rite of passage as a solitary practitioner, you can either skip this step or do it with an eye to one day initiating your own children with the same ritual.

### GIFT(S)

At this point, the Gathering Circle presents gifts to the new young adult. Typically, these gifts represent something about approaching adulthood or increased responsibility.

### GRATITUDE

The Gathering Circle expresses appreciation to the subject for their joining them as a young adult and acknowledges any particular positive characteristics the subject may have (e.g., maturity, caution, patience, etc.).

The new young adult also expresses gratitude for the community and anything else that strikes them in the moment.

### BENEDICTION

The work is declared done, and the new young adult is welcomed with a loud cry of "Welcome, (name)!"

After, the entire group recites: "To enrich and honor the gift of our lives, to chart a kind and true way forward, by these words and deeds we name intent: to dare, to question, to love. May all that must be done, be done in joy. We go forth to live!"

After this ritual, a significant, grounding meal should be shared, both as an experience of fellowship and to fully restore the subject from their fast.

## *Initiation into Adulthood*

An Initiation into Adulthood, frequently conducted around the time a person turns eighteen or prepares to leave home to live on their own, is a time for acknowledgment of the rights and responsibilities a legal adult receives, and for older adults to impart wisdom or experience that can help to guide them in the years when their brains are still forming (until about twenty-five).[11] Often, an "ordeal" of some kind is involved, such as staying up all night to greet the rising Sun.

Similarly to the ritual for Initiation into Young Adulthood, this ritual is conducted by a Circle of Adults—adult friends and loved ones of the subject who will welcome them into adulthood. At this subject's discretion, this may be a group made up only of the subject's own gender if they wish.

### PREPARATION

The subject should dress in clothes in which they feel comfortable and powerful. If they have a ritual outfit, that would be perfect, but clean, neat and attractive ordinary clothing is fine too—even "office formal adult" dress such as suit and tie or a professional dress. They may wish to have a ceremonial bath or shower prior to dressing for the ritual.

### ARRIVAL

First, the Gathering Circle convenes to decorate the room where the ritual will take place (if it is indoors), to discuss how the ritual will go and make sure they have everything ironed out. Holding hands (with consent—opt-out is perfectly fine), they repeat three times:

*We gather to help our loved one, (subject),*
*In their transition to an adult. May we be wise, kind, and honorable,*
*That they may know this as the way of adulthood.*

---

11. Lebel C, Walker L, Leemans A, Phillips L, Beaulieu C. "Microstructural maturation of the human brain from childhood to adulthood." *NeuroImage*. Published online April 2008.

When the subject arrives, they are welcomed and given a seat of honor within the circle. Quiet music may be played, and a small amount of incense burned to create a "magical" environment.

### QUALITIES

Members of the Circle of Adults invoke qualities and characteristics that they hope will be with the subject of the ritual as they go forward. Examples could include maturity, discretion, wisdom, patience, respect, kindness…

### WORKING

- **Narratives:** Each member of the Circle of Adults tells a story in which they were challenged and chose to conduct themselves in an adult manner. They should be sure to include the dilemma—the choice of options, and why they choose the path they did.
- **Charging:** The Circle of Adults assigns (charges) the new adult with responsibility and to live well. If practicing Atheopaganism, this includes honoring of the Four Sacred Pillars and 13 Principles.
- **Acceptance of the Charge:** The subject agrees to follow these precepts to the best of their ability.
- **Declaration:** "Welcome, (subject name), to adulthood!" Shouts the Circle of Adults in unison.
- **Gift(s):** The Circle of Adults gives a gift or gifts to the new adult that symbolize and will be helpful in adulthood.

### GRATITUDE

First, the Circle of Adults expresses appreciation for the new adult. Then the new adult reciprocates.

### BENEDICTION

All participants recite: "To enrich and honor the gift of our lives, to chart a kind and true way forward, by these words and deeds we name intent: to dare, to question, to love. May all that must be done, be done in joy. We go forth to live!"

## Marriage

Marriage is another major life moment for many people. The following are two rites related to this time of life: one for weddings and one for dissolvement.

### *Weddings (Handfasting)*

The following is a synopsis for wedding planning purposes using the ritual structure already provided. Note that most of the rituals described in this book commonly take place in circles of people standing or sitting, rather than in the leader-and-audience model of a church or temple service. In a circle, all are equal, and all are participants, rather than mere witnesses.

Of course, the people you are marrying may want something more mainstream, and you can work with that. But you might start by suggesting a circle-shaped ceremony, with the "action" taking place in the center.

#### ARRIVAL

Arrival is the phase when people settle into the ceremony, open their hearts, and prepare for the emotional experience to come. Arrival can include the declaration of a space of safety and love to enclose the wedding ritual, some welcoming remarks by the officiant, and possibly a *grounding* activity to help participants shake off the stresses and distractions of their travel to the ceremony and ordinary daily concerns. Often, those to be married don't enter the circle until after this "cleansing" has occurred.

#### QUALITIES

The Quality phase is the invocation of those emotions, characteristics, and aspects that the participants in the circle hope to be with them as they conduct the transformative work, or "magic," of the ceremony. In the case of a wedding, it may be an opportunity for the gathered community in the circle to shower the soon-to-be-wed with their wishes for love, kindness, patience, forgiveness, excitement, adventure, sexiness, etc. The couple may wish for you to invoke certain qualities as well, to ensure they are mentioned. If the couple desires to "jump the broom" as a part of their ceremony, you can "concretize" these wishes by having each member of the circle tie a ribbon onto the broom while speaking their wish. The wedding broom will become a treasured keepsake for the couple to preserve after their wedding.

WORKING

The Working is the primary work of the ritual: the wedding ceremony. In most cases, this will involve such traditional elements as the speaking of vows and exchanging of tokens such as rings. Before any declaration of the couple as married, you may wish to ask for affirmation from the community that it is their will that the couple be wed. This can be a moving demonstration of the support among their loved ones for their union. The wedding ceremony itself generally consists of:

- A **procession** of the loved ones of each couple, escorting them to come together in the circle.
- A **welcoming statement** by the officiant, who describes the meaning of marriage and the sacredness of love.
- An invitation to the couple to speak **vows** to one another.
- **Binding of their hands** together with a ceremonial cord, if the couple desires a handfasting ceremony.
- **A "questioning" phase** prior to the declaration of the couple, asking their intentions. The typical "Do you take this man...?" inquiry is an example, but you may ask other questions, such as, "Do you understand the gravity of this act? Do you understand the *levity* of this act?" (many couples simply won't feel it's a "real" wedding if they don't have to say "I do" at some point, so don't disappoint them).
- An invitation to the couple to exchange **tokens of commitment** (such as rings).

- **A declaration that marriage has been achieved:** "By the power invested in me as a cleric of the Atheopagan Society/Universal Life Church minister/etc., I declare you wedded in partnership!" (or wife and wife, or husband and husband, or husband and wife, or whatever the couple has requested they be called in your discussions beforehand).
- There then usually follows a **fervent public display of affection.**

### GRATITUDE

The Gratitude phase occurs after the declaration of marriage. The couple each express their gratitude for whatever they feel is appropriate to recognize at this special time: people, circumstances, life and the Earth itself.

### BENEDICTION

Benediction closes the ritual and sends the participants and the newly married off into the world to live and thrive. Often, this includes:

A presentation to the community of the circle of the newly wedded couple: "To this community I present, the wife and husband Eleanor Cumberbatch and Eliot Bandersnatch!" There will be much cheering.

Additionally, Benediction in a wedding often includes a kind word to the people of the community gathered there, to remember the joy that is living, and kindness, and to carry the love they have witnessed this day forward into the world.

After the Benediction, if the couple wish they can practice the old Pagan tradition of "jumping the broom." A broom is held about a foot above the ground, typically by the Best Man and Maid of Honor, and the wedded couple—with their hands still bound together handfast—run up to and leap over it, to the applause of the wedding guests. Be sure it isn't held too high, or the newlyweds will trip!

Other elements that can be introduced into a wedding ritual at any appropriate point include poetry reading(s), songs or instrumental musical offering (s), a guided meditation, invocation of ancestors, and participation by children.

The ritual is complete, the wedding is done. Time to have a party!

ONE LAST IMPORTANT NOTE:

If you are the officiant at the wedding, at the reception or party following the wedding, be sure to corral the happy couple to have them sign the legal documents, and you sign them yourself. It is generally *your* responsibility as the officiant to deliver these to the proper government office, so be sure you put them in a safe place in the meantime.

## *Dissolution of Marriage*

Divorce rituals are rare in our society, but if those whose marriage is to be dissolved are able and willing, they can provide a sense of closure at the end of a relationship that is no longer working.

Dissolution ceremonies should be short and final. During or before them, rings and family heirlooms should be returned.

Here is an outline for a simple dissolution ceremony for a separating couple. The officiant may have to keep a firm hand on the proceedings if the participants are angry and hurt. The ceremony should include members from the couple's community to support them and witness their dissolution.

PREPARATION

A large, inexpensive glass or ceramic vase of water is prepared, with two empty glasses. A towel large enough to swath the vase and a large rubber band are at hand.

ARRIVAL

Officiant: We are gathered here today to achieve the final separation of the marriage of ____________ and ____________. Friends have joined with us to witness the ending of their time in committed relationship, and to support their moving on to new chapters in their lives.

### QUALITIES

Officiant solicits spoken emotions, values, and characteristics from the participants which they would like to inform the dissolution process, adding such necessary qualities as peace, healing, liberty, and happiness.

### WORKING

If available, a ribbon from the original wedding handfasting ceremony is cast into the vase of water. (If possible—alternatively the wedding rings or some other symbols of the subjects of the ritual may be used.) Officiant states: this is the relationship you have shared.

Officiant then empties the water from the vase in equal amounts into the two glasses and gives one to each member of the couple, saying, now it is time to take yourselves away from what has gone before.

Officiant swathes the vase—now empty except for the ribbon or rings—in the towel, binds the bundle closed with a rubber band, and puts it into the hands (all four) of the divorcing couple. They raise it above their heads and then cast it to the ground to break the vase, formally ending their relationship.

The couple drink their water.

### GRATITUDE

Officiant solicits from each of the divorcing couple an expression of gratitude for their freedom and what they have learned.

### BENEDICTION

It is complete. Officiant declares the work to be done, sending all participants forth to live full, happy, and wise lives.

### NOTES

If wedding rings are used in this ritual, they should be carefully removed from the towel full of broken glass and returned to their owners.

This ritual can be adapted to be done as a solo ritual if the other party is not amenable to participating. Simply pour the glass of water intended for the partner not present as a libation to the Earth, into the ground or on a plant or tree.

## Becoming an Elder

An Eldering, for those who feel they are entering that phase of their lives is a welcoming into a time of wisdom, reduced effort (hopefully) and reflection on what life has brought and taught the person being initiated. This is sometimes a time of giving things away, as in elderhood there is less focus on accumulation and the newly elder person may want to give gifts to the community members in the circle.

### *Eldering Ritual*

This rite can be done at whatever age the person feels they are entering this period time. There is no set age that needs to be reached.

#### ARRIVAL

The subject of the ritual invites a small group of loved ones of the same age or older: the *Wisdom Circle.* Subject welcomes the Wisdom Circle and thanks them for being a part of this transition.

The Wisdom Circle and subject begin the ritual by singing and/or drumming together until they have reached a comfortable, unselfconscious sense of groove and working together.

#### QUALITIES

Wisdom Circle members can call or sing out the qualities they hope to imbue the ritual. Examples might include *Pride in accomplishment. Happiness. Wisdom. Contentment. Humility. Joy in family.*

After the qualities have been invoked, drumming/singing wind down.

#### WORKING

- **Stories:** Each member of the Wisdom Circle recounts a story about the subject which they believe reflects well on their character, maturity and wisdom.

- **Gifts** (optional): Subject gives gifts to members of the Wisdom Circle in thanks for their friendship and support.
- **The Declaration:** Unanimously, the Wisdom Circle says, "For all these reasons, and many more, we recognize you, (name), as an elder in our community! Welcome, and congratulations!"

### GRATITUDE AND BENEDICTION

Wisdom Circle members express thanks to the subject for their great effort in reaching this point in life and achieving all they have achieved.

Subject then expresses gratitude to the Wisdom Circle, and for life itself, and expresses the hope that all go forward in health, happiness, and contentment.

# Chapter 9
# Working with the Dead and Dying

Sometimes, when our friends and family know we are skilled at conducting rituals, we are asked to officiate rites of passage like weddings and funerals. Sometimes that includes being with the dying before they go.

When working with the dying to support them and their loved ones, our role is to listen, to make them as comfortable as possible, to fulfill their wishes for their dying experience as best we are able within the limits of our own boundaries, to support their loved ones through the process, and to identify and work to bring about their wishes for after their death as much as possible.

Dying is a demanding process. Even when pain and discomfort have been minimized, the dying person is going inward, detaching from the world outside themselves. Sitting in silence for long periods is common in working with the dying. But there are often other, more lucid periods when a dying person may want to talk or be able to answer questions about how best to help them. Sometimes they may want company, other times they may wish to be alone.

Key to the experience of being with the dying is not to take anything personally. Dying is a self-focused activity, and especially if they are in pain, the dying may be unkind. But it's not about you, nor should it be—this time is about them. Practice self-care and carefully observe your own boundaries but try to forgive the dying if they hurt your feelings. You would want them to do the same for you.

Many Atheopagans and most other nonbelievers believe that life ends at death, and there is no afterlife. If you believe in some kind of afterlife, you may need to make adjustments to the following material.

## Attending the Grieving

People vary widely in how they relate to death, and to crisis and stress generally. Some loved ones of a dying person may want to talk, some may not. Some may just want someone to watch their kids for a while so they can stay with the dying person or take a walk to get away from the situation for a little while.

Some may want a focus for their anger. And some people simply will not accept that the dying person is dying. The needs vary as widely as do humans of the Earth. Bear in mind that it is unlikely that the loved ones of the dying will all share the same view on death, so you will need to be sensitive to other religious perspectives.

Whatever the family wants, stand up for the dying person's wishes when it comes to content of a planned funeral service. Be gentle, but don't forget that when it comes to their death, it should preferably be on their terms.

Remember your role: you're an adviser. You (probably) aren't a part of the family, and you don't have to pick sides other than to advocate for what the dying person wants. Mostly listening, being helpful, and being sympathetic will get you through. And if you meet implacable opposition to the deceased's wishes from the family, it's all right: the deceased isn't there to witness what happens at that point anyway.

If you find that the family's politics are complicated or bitter, you may want to bring in a professional to help. Suggest a death doula; they specialize in working with the dying and their families. Ask yourself regularly, "Am I in over my head here?" and if the answer is yes, find a more experienced person to step in or to advise you.

## After a Death

While it is not your role to tell grieving loved ones how to proceed with funerary rites and disposal of the body, you can be helpful to them by making certain that they understand their rights and options. Funerals can be a severe financial burden on many grieving families, especially if they allow themselves to be sold expensive options by a funeral home. Suggested affordable and low-impact funeral homes and many resources on death and dying can be found at the nonprofit Order of the Good Death website.

Grieving families should know that embalming is not a legal or health requirement, and once the body has been released by the coroner's office, they may claim it themselves for a home funeral. Families have the option of taking possession of the body themselves for washing, viewing, etc. prior to burial or cremation, and there are many eco-friendly burial alternatives which are not only better for the Earth, but they are also better for the survivors' pocketbooks. Loved ones and families should understand that if they do not want the involvement of a funeral home, they do not have to have it...whatever a funeral home might tell them. They may want to involve a funeral home for a cremation but leave everything else to themselves and loved ones. You can help enormously simply by volunteering to call funeral homes and get quotes for the services the loved ones want—prices can vary widely from business to business.

### *Considerations*

Immediately after you become aware of the death, whether you just received the news by phone or if you are present with the body, if at all possible do nothing. Don't run off to make phone calls and arrangements. Sit quietly. Feel the moment. Be with the solemn reality of human mortality. Hold the departed in your heart with fondness.

If loved ones need support you can offer, of course you should provide it to them. But if you can, take the time to reflect on the life that has ended, all those moments, activities, memories.

And then turn to the business of contacting those who must be contacted, addressing the legalities, arranging for disposition of the body, and planning for funerary rites.

In organizing funerary rites, there are several considerations to keep in mind:

- What kind of ritual is it? A small, intimate blessing of the body with the closest loved ones? A graveside or pre-cremation service? A community memorial ceremony with all the friends and loved ones of the deceased? Examples of each of these are provided in the following material.
- Are there any politics? Are there loved ones who should be kept away from one another? Are there religious difference that need to be known about or respected?
- How many participants will there be?
- Will the ritual be indoors, or out? If the latter, what if the weather doesn't cooperate?

## Format of Death Rites

Your ritual honoring and commemoration of a person who has died could take many forms, depending on the needs and details of the situation. If you have been asked to preside over a death rite, take care to solicit important information from key family members as you design the ritual. Remember at all times that death rites are for the living: they are intended to help bring closure, catharsis and acknowledgment of the death for those who loved the deceased. As you design the ritual, start with the question of how people are to be arranged for it.

### *Circular (or "Pagan") Format*

A circular layout of your ritual space can emphasize the communal nature of the funeral and help everyone see the community gathered there. It also makes ritual elements like calling Qualities easier and may also reduce unease among some who have escaped from an authoritarian religious background. A circular type of ritual may be framed by "drawing a circle" or "quarter calls" and will be more interactive than a sermon type service.

Pagan rituals generally take place in circles, but there are limits to how many people you can organize in a circle, depending on available space and location. Sometimes you can gather people in a circle more than one person deep, but if so, don't plan for people to hold hands or pass objects around during the ritual, because they will never figure it out.

### *Church Service Format*

A regular church layout is what many of us are familiar with. In addition to having a church type layout (with the chairs in rows all facing the front, where the podium is), the ritual might be configured similarly to a typical church service, with speakers facing an audience of mourners. If the ritual will be really large—say, more than one hundred people—it becomes more practical to use an indoor space with ranks of seats, though you can also do multiple ranks of chairs in a circle. As with all large rituals, keep it simple and remember that people are grieving. They mostly want to receive an experience, not to create one. But be sure there are roles for loved ones who want them.

### *Remember to Consider Your Participants*

Don't make participants stand for long periods. Provide chairs so they can sit comfortably and make a designated space for wheelchairs and for other people with accessibility needs. Be considerate of expected temperatures and precipitation. If there are to be frail participants, perhaps a comfortable indoor location is best.

## Funerary Rites

Following are three rituals to honor the dead. The first is a body blessing for a home funeral. The second is a rite to remember to be performed at any appropriate time. The third is a celebration of life to be done after a formal funeral.

### *Funerary Rite I: Body Blessing for a Home Funeral*

Typically occurring shortly after death (or after the body is brought home from the hospital or coroner's office, where it will rest until the time for disposal), this is generally the smallest and most intimate funerary rite. Preparing the body for eventual disposal is a final act of loved by the survivors of the deceased: a caring for the body that was the person and is no longer. It is a profound and beautiful way of saying goodbye.

There is no formal structure for such a rite. Elements often include washing the body, washing, and brushing or setting the hair, anointing with scented oils (earthy scents such as cedar and sandalwood, or the deceased's favorite scent are appropriate), placing jewelry on the body if desired, and (if there is to be no viewing/visitation) wrapping the body in cloth or a shroud. If the deceased wished to be buried clothed, this is the time to dress them.

If you are anxious at the prospect of such a ritual, consider hiring a death doula to assist. They understand how to work with the dead and their families and can be a great partner in working with a grieving family.

I have participated in these rituals, and they are vivid, solemn, loving and kind. They help the loved ones to come to grips with the reality of the death, which is one step toward, if not acceptance of it, at least peaceful acknowledgment of it.

If viewing and visitation are to take place, the body may be put in a bed with ice packs and/or dry ice atop and underneath it, to slow decomposition. The body can be maintained like this—particularly if there are air conditioning and cool conditions—for a day or two. If you are concerned about leakage, use a rubber hospital sheet under the fitted sheet. Check with your local laws; many places require un-embalmed bodies to be buried or cremated within three days of death.

A viewing chamber may be decorated with photos, mementos, etc., and so forth. You may want to burn a small amount of aromatic herbs or incense in the (unlikely) case of decomposition odors—frankincense, dragon's blood resin, and sage are all appropriate. A rolled cloth or small towel may be placed under the chin of the body to keep the mouth from dropping open, which some may find disturbing.

## *Funerary Rite II: Circle of Remembrance (Graveside/Ash-Scattering Service)*

This form of funerary rite may be conducted either in the presence of the body at burial, or after the body has been buried or cremated. It is a ceremony for the loved ones of the deceased to acknowledge that their loved one has gone back into the Earth and is now an honored memory (recognition and celebration of life for the broader community is discussed later in this section).

The celebrants gather in a circle. If a burial service, circle around the grave or shrouded/casketed body; if not, circle around the receptacle holding the ashes, or the area where ashes are to be scattered, commemorative plants are to be planted and/or a monument is to be erected. If, for some reason, the deceased's remains are not present, celebrants may circle around a memorial Focus of objects reminiscent of the deceased.

### ARRIVAL

The Arrival phase may include a meditation on the gift of life, and the statement that now we return the remains of our loved one to the Earth from which they came.

### QUALITIES

The Qualities invoked may include remembrance, love, grief, regret, and so forth.

#### WORKING

Working may include activities such as:

- Lowering the casket or body by hand into the grave
- Burying the casket or body by hand (either completely or partially, leaving the rest to be done by cemetery attendants)
- Planting seeds, bulbs, or a sapling
- Decorating the grave / erecting a monument
- Scattering ashes

#### GRATITUDE

The Gratitude phase may acknowledge thankfulness for the loved one's life, for loving community, and for the gift of life itself.

#### BENEDICTION

Benediction closes the ritual with a reminder of the rarity and preciousness of life, and the wish that celebrants may bear this grief with strength, self-compassion and warm remembrance.

### *Funerary Rite III: A Celebration of Life*

This form of funerary rite may be conducted weeks or even months after the death, enabling all family and community members who choose to attend to plan for the event and travel to reach it.

#### GATHERING / ARRIVAL / QUALITIES

Play music that was loved by the deceased during this period (or as chosen by the parent(s), if this is a stillbirth or miscarriage memorial). It doesn't have to be sad music! A memorial is a celebration of a life. Have pictures of the deceased liberally distributed throughout the welcoming area.

#### WORKING

You begin with welcoming remarks by you. Bid everyone welcome and ask them to be seated. Welcome the family in particular, and if there are any "dignitaries" or special friends to the family, welcome them, too. Have everyone take a deep breath and blow it out and say something like: "We are here, in this place today, in the presence of the profound reality that is death. In our sorrow, we come together today to celebrate the life of (name of the deceased)." Other activities may include:

- **Poem or prose reading celebrating the gift of life:** This is a reminder of the beauty of life on Earth, in this extraordinary Cosmos. That we live here, surrounded by wonders, for a brief time, and then dissolve back into the Cosmos from which we arose.
- **Musical interlude:** A song or instrumental piece—guests may be invited to sing along if the organizers wish it. Be sure to provide music sheets to guests if you choose this option.
- **Eulogy:** A prepared speech to memorialize and celebrate the life of the deceased. Usually delivered by a family member or close friend. May include description of the deceased's spirituality and what it meant to them, and/or any final words the deceased left behind for their community.
- **Poem or prose reading:** Some good secular choices are available at https://www.bustle.com/articles/152207-16-non-religious-funeral-readings-from-poems.
- **Open mike to share memories of the deceased:** spontaneous memories are shared by guests.
- **Musical interlude:** another song or instrumental piece, possibly with guests singing.

BENEDICTION

A closing statement by the officiant acknowledging the love and respect that has been expressed for the deceased, gratitude for the deceased's life, with well-wishes for the family and loved ones, an adjuration to embrace our precious lives, and an invitation to the reception following the memorial, if any (and/or burial service if that is to follow).

Restart gathering music as attendees stand and prepare to leave.

Chapter 10

# Personal and Healing Rituals

The cyclical celebrations and rites of passage described in the previous sections both identify "milestones" in life, when the passage of time has brought us to recognize that change has occurred. However, there are many other opportunities for ritual observances, both for rites of passage that don't line up with these occasions, and for more personal needs.

Some of these—like a healing ritual to address psychological wounding or to build confidence for a job search—are described here, but you can use the ritual format provided previously to do a ritual intended for any purpose. You may find, as I have, that when I need an emotional shot in the arm, a ritual is my go-to approach.

## Transition Rites

A *transition rite* is a rite of passage in which the participants and subject either perform or acknowledge a major and likely permanent change in the subject. Examples might include a deconstruction out of an authoritarian religious tradition, or a transformation from being a working person to entering retirement, a political transformation to a new viewpoint, the beginning of a new spiritual path or the beginning of a new career. In a transition rite, the subject of the ritual enters in one state, and through the process of the transforming ritual changes into another.

Alternatively, the ritual may be more of a welcoming into the new state, having already left the old. This is a decision up to the subject of the ritual.

While it is probably better to do transition rituals in a group format, so the person undergoing the transformation is seen and recognized as having made the shift, this ritual can also be designed as a solitary one.

As I cannot directly speak from the experience of those who might choose a transition rite for these examples, rather than present a ritual based on no knowledge, I present here a short list of ingredients which can be selected from by those designing such a ritual for themselves or another. Design your ritual using the format discussed previously and incorporating any of the following elements into the Working phase. These are just a few; I am sure there are many other elements which might be included in such a list:

- **Crossing the line.** in which a physical line is established in the middle of the ritual space and the subject steps across it to their new state of being. Friends and family can be on the new side to welcome the subject to their new state.
- **Changing uniforms.** which can be as all-encompassing as completely stripping down and then putting on clothing that reflects the new state, or as simple as to take off one kind of hat and put on another. A more elaborate example might be to have the subject's hair cut in a new style that reflects their new state, right in the ritual space (make sure you have someone who knows what they are doing!)
- **Ritual washing.** in which a basin of water and a towel are provided to "wash off" the old state. May be followed by anointing with a scent or other forms of symbolically "putting on" the new state.

- **Equipping.** In this ritual activity, the subject is ceremonially presented with tools and symbols of their new state. In the case of a retirement, for example, a subject who loves to fish might be presented with a new rod and reel, or the classic, a gold watch.
- **The value swap.** In this activity, a symbolic "trade" is made in which the values of the old state are swapped for those of the new. In the case of a religious deconstruction, this could be to swap obedience, submission, belief in inherent sin, etc., for new values of self-esteem, agency, belief in the basic decency of most people, etc.
- **The self-affirmation.** Many transitions are out of identities with which the subject no longer identifies (sinful, broken, obedient, etc.) and into new ones (proud, effective, lovable, independent, etc.) A deliberate phase of the Working in many such rituals focuses on affirming this shift and declaring the subject of the ritual to be identified by the new descriptors, supplanting the old.
- **Joining the group.** In this ritual activity, the subject is welcomed by a group of people who have already undergone the transition now being marked by the subject.

Transition rituals can be extraordinarily impactful and important for their subjects, marking the beginning of an entire new chapter in their lives. It is a privilege to help to develop and conduct one for a loved one or member of your community.

## Healing Rituals

We all have challenges: psychological wounds from trauma, abuse, neglect, loss or hardship. Humans have conducted healing rituals for many thousands of years to help one another get through them. Rituals are powerful processes which can help us to recover from trauma, to come to terms with grief and loss, and to rewrite internal narratives about ourselves, humanity, and life itself. We can conduct healing rituals by ourselves, or with groups of trusted loved ones.

Another important note: Healing rituals heal everyone who participates. Even if you are not the focus of such a ritual, the simple human compassion, kindness, and generosity of working to ease another's pain will serve your own heart as well.

One important note: rituals are *not* a replacement for medical or psychiatric care. They can boost and support us psychologically but if you are ill or injured—physically or mentally—seek qualified medical attention.

## *Full Healing Ritual*

Healing rituals must be designed with great care. We must not discount the profound impact they can have upon the vulnerable person who has opened themselves to transformation and growth.

I will walk through the specifics of the phases in this kind of ritual and then provide some examples.

### PREPARATION

Is the healing recipient ready to go through the ritual process? Are the other participants? A preparatory shower or bath for the recipient may be prescribed, with scented soap or oil if desired. The recipient may want to fast for the day leading up to the ritual, consuming only water and/or fruit juice or broth.

### ARRIVAL

In the Arrival phase of the ritual, what is essential is creating a safe container of love and witnessing. Decorate the ritual space to be attractive to the recipient and contain reminders—*not* traumatic reminders—of the circumstances of their wounding. Make sure the temperature is comfortable, and the light level is low but not so low that participants cannot see one another's faces. Possibly have someone keep a slow drumbeat or have appropriate ritual music. Have a blanket at hand in case the subject of the ritual feels a need to cover themselves or "hide."

#### DECLARATION OF INTENTION

At this point in the ritual, it is important to state explicitly the purpose of the ritual. The subject of the ritual formally asks for help with their challenge; the other participants express their willingness to help.

#### INVOCATION OF QUALITIES

The focus of the ritual declares their intention in undergoing this ritual. The rest of the participants express their commitment to support that person in their healing work.

#### WORKING

As always, this should be a symbolic activity which enacts the transformation of the wounding events. Examples may include a laying on of hands by participants or gathering around the subject to hold them close; it could be a feedback circle of participants telling the subject how valued and loved they are.

Be creative! Ritual space is rather like dreaming: anything can be possible and what you present to the subject should grip and fascinate them, as well as being emotionally cathartic.

#### GRATITUDE

On the part of the subject of the healing, this is acknowledgment that the transformation sought has been achieved—the ritual has worked! Participants can also chime in with their own reasons for gratitude.

#### BENEDICTION

Closing the ritual should include commitments of support from each participant to the recipient, to help them continue with their healing.

### *Get Creative*

As I said when first describing this ritual format, there are many others, and I encourage you to experiment. However, this outline creates an effective experiential arc and can be relied on if you are uncertain of how to structure your healing ritual.

As an example, my ritual circle, Dark Sun, once performed a healing ritual in which we performed mock surgery on a member to "remove" a physical representation of a parasitic family member; another time, we created an actual grave in which the subject needed to dig to find things she thought had long been lost to her, like her resolve and courage. Following are three examples of healing rituals I have done, sometimes repeatedly.

### *The Atheopagan Rosary*

I find that—when I can make myself do it—a daily mindfulness meditation adds a great deal to my experience of living. I created a set of meditation beads (or "rosary") to facilitate repeated mental affirmations.

I drew the meditation for this rosary from Buddhist sources cited in a mindfulness class I took, as well as the 13 Principles of Atheopaganism as I practice them. You can write your own, of course, for seasonal holidays or other uses. But the main point is the use of repetition to reprogram your brain to embrace the qualities in the meditation: to make a better world for you, for those around you, and for all of us.

If you're like me, be ready for a lot of internal chatter disputing these statements—that's why they're powerful. With time, that fades, and you start to experience the meditation's statements as true.

The bead string itself is simple: three courses of thirteen beads, with the thirteenth always being recognizable as the last of a series. I like beautiful things, so I went to a bead store and bought pretty beads mostly of fused glass, seashells, etc.; they feel solid and weighty in the hand. A larger one could certainly be made; I like prime numbers, so if I were going to make a bigger rosary, I would probably go for seven courses (ninety-one beads). I place the rosary on my Focus when it isn't in use.

To say the rosary, speak or think one line for each bead. I go through the following meditation three times (three repetitions of the three courses):

| FIRST TWO COURSES OF 13 | LAST COURSE OF 13 |
|---|---|
| *May my heart be happy* | *My heart is happy* |
| *May my mind be at ease* | *My mind is at ease* |
| *May my body be healthy* | *My body is healthy* |
| *May I know peace today* | *Peace is with me today* |
| *May those I touch know kindness* | *I am kind to those around me* |
| *May the Cosmos be honored* | *The Cosmos fills me with wonder* |
| *May the good Earth be revered* | *The good Earth is generous* |
| *May my heart be grateful* | *My heart is grateful* |
| *May I act with integrity* | *I act with integrity* |
| *May I know that I am loved* | *I am loved* |
| *That I deserve love* | *I deserve love* |
| *That all deserve love* | *All deserve love* |
| *May all I am and do, be of love* | *All I am and do is of love* |
| (repeat) | |

## The Jewel

This is a solitary ritual for personal growth and healing work. It is especially recommended for those who struggle with self-esteem due to past abuse or neglect.

Arrange a Focus with a mirror in the center, flanked by candles, and a cup or chalice of wine or flavorful juice. Burn a delicious-smelling incense: I recommend Russian Orthodox incense (available at most Orthodox bookstores) for this ritual. It may help to print the meditations on little cards and prop them against the bottom of the mirror so you can read them while maintaining your gaze on your reflection.

Close your eyes and concentrate on your breath going in and out, your clothes shifting as your chest rises and falls. Breathe deeply from the belly. Feel where gravity holds you down against the Earth. Drink the good air and know it is a gift, a sustaining gift of the World to you. Wait until you are calm and centered, then open your eyes.

Gaze into your eyes in the mirror. Speak this meditation slowly and with measured cadence:

"You are a jewel. Many facets, unique, an artwork of the Universe.

You are perfect. You are as you should be, in this moment.

You are loved. You are worthy of love.

You are a jewel. No other could replace you. You are welcome here."

Repeat seven times. You may feel tension and resistance as you say these words, because parts of you don't believe them. That's okay—the point of this ritual is to strengthen the parts that do.

After the seventh time, take and let out a deep breath. Then say,

> *"I am a jewel. I am unique, an artwork of the Universe.*
>
> *I am perfect. I am as I should be, in this moment.*
>
> *I am loved. I am worthy of love.*
>
> *I am a jewel. I belong here."*
>
> Repeat three times.

Close by sipping the wine or juice until it is gone. Know that this pleasure, this gift is your birthright: you deserve happiness.

### *The Absolution*

This deceptively simple ritual can be profoundly impactful for participants, so be sure to establish a solidly safe container for the ritual before proceeding to the Working.

After the Arrival and Qualities phases, officiant urges participants to close their eyes and call forth their most embarrassing and shameful memory, the first that comes to mind—something that makes their chests crawl when they think about it—and to hold that memory and feeling in the forefront of their minds.

Then, the officiant absolves each of them, one by one, working their way around the circle. This may be done a couple of ways.

- **With anointment:** Officiant asks each participant in turn, "Are you ready to transform this feeling? May I touch your forehead?"

On receiving consent, officiant dips a finger in a chalice of water, and draws three circles on the forehead of the participant, saying: "You are pure. You are absolved. You are clean. It's gone!" Officiant then moves on to the next participant. Be sure to ask permission to touch each participant before doing so.

- **Without anointment:** Officiant asks each participant in turn, "Are you ready to transform this feeling? May I touch your forehead?" On receiving consent, officiant touches the forehead of the participant firmly, saying: "You are pure. You are absolved. You can let it go. It's gone!" Officiant then moves on to the next participant. Be sure to ask permission to touch each participant before doing so.

After all participants have been absolved, officiant invites participants to express gratitude for anything in their life they feel grateful for. Officiant begins by expressing thankfulness for this circle and the courage, vulnerability and openness shared by the participants.

Officiant offers a benediction, sending the participants out into the world lighter, freer, happier, to spread this sense of lightness and freedom to others.

After this emotionally intense ritual it is recommended that participants do grounding activities like eating some food or placing palms or the soles of the feet against the ground for a few minutes. If they continue to feel light-headed or "otherworldly," continue these activities until they feel normal again before driving a car or otherwise operating heavy machinery.

It is remarkable how impactful it can be to receive simple permission from another human being to divest oneself of a deep-seated shame and guilt. Some participants have had tears running down their faces as I absolved them of their past shameful acts through this ritual.

## Special Rituals When You Need Them

Sometimes, you just need to get unstuck: say, you're looking for a job, or you have writer's block. Or you need help. Or life feels boring. Or you need patience for dealing with a difficult situation. Or you feel overwhelmed by some upcoming event and you want to be strong and capable for it.

Your ritual practice can help with those things. You can draw on your practice and skills to help craft rituals intended to boost confidence, heal psychological wounds, bring a sense of calm even when life is chaos. Sometimes an angry ritual like a *banishing* or a *hex* can feel good, just to vent and get the raw emotion out of your system!

It's rare for me to develop special rituals just for such needs, but I have done them and they have been effective in shifting my mood and perspective. Whether it's tucking a sigil into my breast pocket for a job interview, lighting a candle for strength or doing serious healing work in the mirror, rituals can help us to be more whole and mentally healthy, and to perform well under pressure.

Remember those "lucky" rituals by athletes that I referenced at the beginning of the book? These are the kinds of rituals that help those folks to perform at their very peak capability.

Use the ritual format provided in Section 3, "Ritual Basics," and design an experience for yourself that will focus your intention and concentration on your goal. You will be amazed how much better you will feel when you have done so.

Here are a couple of solitary ritual outlines as examples of personal rituals which can be conducted as needed:

## *To Increase Focus for a Job Search*

Being unemployed can wreak havoc on a person's self-esteem, sense of purpose and financial condition. Paradoxically, it is when challenged in these ways that we must be our most confident in submitting applications, writing cover letters and interviewing.

This ritual is a way to help bolster personal confidence under pressure.

### PREPARATION

Print out a copy of your resume. Have a candle, a means to light it, a coin (preferably a valuable one) and a piece of green ribbon ready to hand. (The green is for money, but if you associate a different color with money, use that). You can also use a pay stub from a previous job, so long as you don't have a negative association with that job.

Set out these materials and any symbols of your work and career that feel appropriate in a simple Focus for this ritual. Light some incense to help create a magical atmosphere.

### ARRIVAL

Light the candle and conduct your usual Arrival techniques to enter the ritual state of trance.

### QUALITIES

Invoke the Qualities of right livelihood, enjoyable work, good pay and benefits, confidence and self-assuredness, effective communication, and presentation skills.

### WORKING

To begin with, pass the coin through the incense smoke and place it in a prominent place on your Focus.

Next, roll up your resume with your name at the top visible on the outside of the roll. Say, "I empower this document to persuade, excite and attract my future employer. May I be filled with confidence as I interview for a new job and may I effectively communicate how perfect I would be for that position!"

Now wrap the ribbon around the rolled-up resume several times and cross the ends over one another. Drip wax from the candle onto the crossed ends to seal the package shut and say, "It is done! This magic is sealed!"

### GRATITUDE

Name things from your life you are grateful for, particularly in relation to work and employment, as well as gratitude for the new job that is coming.

#### BENEDICTION

Say, "This work is complete. I go forward to do the work of gaining this new work, with thanks to the good Earth for all that it pours out for me. Onward!" Blow out the candle. Place the sealed resume on your Focus and carry the coin with you as a talisman to job interviews and other related activities. The ritual is complete.

### *To Instill a Sense of Safety and Protection*

This secular rendition of a spell jar is a confidence-booster for the security, happiness, and safety of your home.

#### PREPARATION

Gather the following materials: a pint or half-pint mason jar with a sealable lid; sealing wax or a taper candle of a color that symbolizes peace and happiness to you; several metal nails and/or thumbtacks (no plastic, please); red wine vinegar, enough to fill the jar; You can also include a slip of paper with a sigil that you have prepared in advance on the theme of "protection, safety and happiness." See page 84 for sigil creation.

Lay out a focus with these items and symbols that mean safety and protection to you.

#### ARRIVAL

Light the candle and conduct whatever usual Arrival practices you use to bring yourself into the ritual state.

#### QUALITIES

Invoke the qualities of fierceness, protectiveness, courage, strength, security, and a happy home.

#### WORKING

Place the nails/thumbtacks in the jar, repeating as you do so "with this act, I protect my home from unwanted occurrences, summoning joy and contentment and happy days" three times. Fill the jar with vinegar, and then introduce the sigil if you are using one.

Put the lid on the jar and then seal it with sealing wax or wax from the candle. Let cool.

### GRATITUDE

Speak your gratitude for the safety and happiness you are invoking for yourself and your household.

### BENEDICTION

Now, go outside and bury the jar next to your front gate, or the main entrance to your home.

Declare, "By my will and intention, may this symbol hold vigil over our home and selves, keeping us safe and well." Then go inside and blow the candle out, ending the ritual.

# Chapter 11
# Building Community for Sharing Rituals

It's perfectly fine to have a solitary spiritual practice. You can cultivate a rich relationship with the cycles of life in your region and learn a lot about yourself, your world and what makes you happy.

That said, humans are social creatures. Most of us like to do things together. And ritual celebrations are particularly rich, moving, and wonderful when they are shared with friends and loved ones. This being the case, here are some suggestions for finding others who would like to explore this journey of adventure with you.

First of all, you don't need to use "controversial" labels as you seek out newcomers to share your experiences with you. Even if you are a nonbeliever or a Pagan, you needn't say "atheist" or "Pagan" in doing so. You can simply put out the word—say, on MeetUp.com, which is a great tool for finding people of similar interests—that you want to start having secular seasonal celebrations and are looking for people to share them. The word "secular" is more benign than "non-religious" or certainly "atheistic"—try that and see how it works for you.

I suggest an introductory meeting at a neutral space like a reserved meeting room at a local library prior to inviting anyone to your home. Such meetings can involve introductions, icebreaker activities and your presentation of an overview of the kinds of events you want to start holding. Then you can choose from those who show up for who you want to invite to your gatherings.

Such gatherings can begin with a short statement, poem, or food blessing thanking the Earth and Sun for their bounty, and perhaps a ceremonial lighting of candles to welcome new friends and acquaintances. My favorite food blessing is:

> *"This food, swelling from the Earth by the breath of the Sun, is brought to us by many hands. May all be honored."*
> *Attendees reply in unison: "We are grateful to eat today."*

Another place you can seek like-minded new friends is in Unitarian Universalist congregations near you. Many non-theists and agnostics attend UU services, appreciating the sense of community as well as their values and social justice efforts. Posting an announcement on a UU community bulletin board will probably draw some interest. Note that some UU congregations also have chapters of CUUPs—the Covenant of Unitarian Universalist Pagans—who will be familiar with the Wheel of the Year and doing rituals. While many CUUPs practitioners are theistic, many are not as well, and will probably be happy to join you in your secular celebrations.

Finally, there are Pagan organizations in many areas, and you can reach out to them, too, letting them know that you are seeking to celebrate naturalistic or non-theistic Pagan holidays with like-minded folks and inviting them to contact you.

Other folks who may be interested in celebrating rituals with you may be found among participants in the Burning Man festival or its related regional "burns." Many have message boards online you can access to put out your call.

## Chosen Family

Not all of us have the benefit of families that support us for who we are, whether that's our political values, our gender, our sexuality, our spiritual path or simply our personality. It is intensely painful to be rejected on the basis of these so-personal characteristics, as they go to the very core of who we are.

In some cases, in fact, the best approach to dealing with family members who claim to love us but are hostile to who we are is simply to stop having an approach: to minimize or even eliminate contact with these family members. This can be painful and sad—many benefit from therapy and/or grief rituals when making such a decision.

I speak from experience with this; my family was so intensely toxic and hostile to who I am that eventually I stopped dealing with them entirely. My life got better. And over time, I came to understand that this is really their loss.

Now, is there residual pain and longing when such a severance takes place? Of course there is. Particularly, we can long for an idealized "Mother" or "Father" that isn't the actual people who are in these roles in our lives. That longing takes a very long time to fade.

But the good news about setting boundaries around family members who are not supportive of who you are is that it creates space for *chosen family.*

It is not uncommon for people who practice ritual together to become very intimate over time, and to come to have familial-style relationships with one another. I have been blessed to be a part of the ritual circle Dark Sun since 1991, and they are now the only family I know.

I include this advisory because you want to be very deliberate about the people you pursue a small group ritualizing relationship with. Make sure they are people you feel good about.

They might end up being your chosen family.

## What to Look for in a Co-Ritualist

Sharing rituals can be an intimate thing. Over time, people who share rituals learn personal details about one another: about their histories, their psychological issues, their temperaments, their relationships. You want to have confidence that those you share these things with are worthy of the confidence. So here are a few things to look for:

- **Sense of humor:** Good humor and an ability to take challenges in stride are indicators that a person is generally mentally healthy.
- **Critical thinking:** An ability to discern likely fact from fiction is essential not only to be grounded in reality, but to process conflict reasonably.
- **Ability to keep a confidence:** Trustworthiness with private information is essential for members of a ritual group.
- **Intention to grow as a person:** Secular spirituality is about exploration, both of the world and of the self. Someone who is highly defensive or in denial about their personal issues is likely to find themselves challenged by an ongoing ritual practice. Owning one's feelings, reaction patterns, etc. is essential in a balanced person and good co-ritualist.

You can test the waters with new people by holding open (anyone welcome) ritual events for a while and then inviting good prospects to a by-invitation-only event. Be sure to capture email addresses or phone numbers at your open events or you won't know how to reach people!

## Considerations and Cautions for Working in Groups

It can feel wonderful to find a group of people with whom you can share your ritual practice. Whether it's a local Pagan group, or a group recruited through MeetUp or simply by putting the word out to your like-minded friends, there can truly be a sense of "coming home" as you incorporate regular observances into your life; a feeling like you have found something precious that you never knew you were missing so much.

But there are considerations to keep in mind. Group dynamics can be tricky, especially if there are personalities that want to dominate or "be the leader."

My recommendation is to join (or start) groups where the power structure is flat: where there is no hierarchy of "priesthood" or "senior members" or "founders" who have higher status than do newer members. If you are the founder of a group, you may be surprised at how tempting it can be to remain a central and "more important" figure rather than just another member of an egalitarian group. Don't do it!

Groups dominated by one or more strong personalities tend to implode, as resentment over power differential simmers and eventually boils over. And in the worst cases, if the group doesn't fall apart, genuinely cult-like behavior can start to emerge.

### *Cult Indicators*

People who are in a cult often don't know they are in a cult.

Cult-like conditions can accumulate slowly until factors that disempower members to the benefit of leaders are in place. Here are ten factors to look for in determining whether a group has cult-like attributes:

- One or more **charismatic leader(s)** who cannot be challenged or questioned.
- Deceptive **recruitment tactics.**
- **Exclusivity:** members are not allowed to belong to other groups or faiths.
- Intimidation, Fear, Shame and/or Isolation are used to **punish nonconformity.**
- **Religious dogma** that must be followed.
- **Sexual abuse or manipulation:** Leaders are sexually involved with lower-status members or sexual acts are expected in exchange for elevated status in the group.

- Emphasis is placed on **recruiting vulnerable people** such as those who have recently experienced loss, who are in challenging survival circumstances or have health issues.
- **Insularity:** encouraging members to engage only with other members, even sometimes to the point of renouncing their families and previous friends.
- **Financial exploitation** of members.
- **Lack of transparency** about decisions and particularly finances of the group.

Any of these attributes is a sign of a group you probably don't want to be a part of. More than one is a serious red flag. Things don't have to be that way: steer clear and find a group where you are supported, encouraged, and empowered.

## Assessing Group Dynamics

When assessing a group, ask yourself, "Do people seem happy here? Do they seem grounded in reality? Are science and critical thinking celebrated? Do members' lives seem healthy and balanced? Are people kind and mutually supportive? If there are leader figures, are they accountable to the membership?" The answers to these questions not only tell you whether there are any red flags around cultism, but also whether it's a group that you are likely to find a home in. Don't settle!

# Chapter 12
# Beyond Rituals: Living the Spiritual Life

Up to this point, this book has been about techniques you can use to have a richer, happier life filled with moments of meaning and joy, through development of a ritual practice. And that's great. People being happier is a worthy goal, in and of itself.

But there is more to be had, if we choose it: as we grow, change, learn and age, we can become wiser.

It's a word that makes some of us cringe a little: *wisdom*. Because pretty much anyone who claims to have it is automatically suspicious, right?

It's those who *don't* claim to have it who very often do.

My contention is this: if you are living in a manner open to growth and change, the trade-off for the physical infirmities that come with age is the accumulation of wisdom: of internal tools so that you are able to contend calmly with adversity, of a big-picture perspective that helps you not to sweat the small stuff. And the recognition that nearly all of it is, in the end, small stuff.

Wisdom comes with experience: experience in relating with others, in exploring the unique configurations of the self, in navigating life's challenges, in learning how to find happiness and contentment in the course of living. Wisdom brings a deep understanding of priorities, with love and kindness outweighing such things as acquisition of wealth. And it teaches us patience.

It is, like all things, not perfect. And we don't always live in our wisdom: when triggered, when angry, when defensive we may do or say things that our wisdom knows will be counterproductive. But we do them anyway ... and thus accumulate a little more experience that may help us to be wiser the next time.

My path, Atheopaganism, is a path about joy, connection and wisdom. It encourages us to know ourselves, to cultivate wise values, to celebrate love and the many pleasures of this life and to help the world to be kinder and more responsible.

So don't undersell your own wisdom. It's there, whether or not you can access it at any given moment. With experience, it will come more readily to hand.

It's growing as you do. Cultivate it. Listen to that calm, experienced voice in your head, however weak it may seem.

Grow to be wiser. At the end of the day, it will bring you deeper contentment than any material pleasures. It will add to the lives of those around you.

It will contribute to the creation of a better, kinder world.

That's what this section is about.

## How Do We Become Wiser?

Those of us practicing this form of spirituality are about being healthier, wiser, happier humans, and through action contributing to a better world.

Some of that is about values. Those of Atheopaganism are articulated in the 4 Sacred Pillars and the 13 Atheopagan Principles, and in this area particularly Principle 4: humility; Principle 5: perspective and humor; Principle 7: inclusiveness; Principle 8: legacy; Principle 9: social responsibility, and especially Principle 13: kindness and compassion.

But whether or not you choose to adopt these Principles and to call yourself an Atheopagan, it really doesn't matter. What matters is that you grow, heal, and unfold into the magnificence that is inherent in you.

Some of that is about healing: **healing your wounds and shame,** your damaged **self-esteem.** Your **fear.**

And some of it is about moving through and beyond your personal nonsense.

Which, let us be clear, we all have: rationalizations, excuse-making, denial, self-deception and willful ignoring of things we don't want to look at.

Personal work is core and essential work. And if we seek to be wise, complete people, a willingness to confront our biases, our truisms, our histories of injury—and, yes, our egoism, mistaken understandings, and blind spots—and to transform these into wisdom and compassion is a part of what the path requires of us.

Will any of us accomplish this perfectly? No, we will not.

That's why it's called a path instead of a destination.

The self alone is not the focus of Atheopaganism. The personal community, human society, and the ecological systems of the Earth are priorities as well for our service and attention. But just as it is erroneous to focus on nothing but the self to the exclusion of the communal and ecological, it is a mistake to ignore personal growth as an aspect of a healthy, fulfilling way of being.

We have all been wounded. We have all absorbed destructive culture and learned inappropriate behavior. We have suffered. We grieve, we rage. It is the human experience.

Knowing yourself and working to grow is a lifelong journey. Sometimes growth happens in leaps; sometimes it is so incremental that you can hardly tell it is happening until you turn around one day and realize: *I've changed.*

It is immensely rewarding, and tremendously humbling. It humanizes us, helps us to see how each of us struggles with mental demons and damage.

And it gives us the foundation of warmth and compassion from which can spring activism to better the world for all of us... with "us" meaning not only humans, but the fabric of life itself.

As you create a personal practice that can help you to reflect and grow and celebrate, journal your thoughts and feelings, and learn from them. Read the words of people who have worked hard to become increasingly kind and compassionate: from Thich Nhat Hanh to Pema Chodron to Nelson Mandela, they are out there.

Each of us has a life to live and a self and world to improve. This is the human project. Let us embrace it and do the work to make progress, day by day.

## Three Big Lessons

I believe there are three core lessons that are the foundation to a wise life: *the Big OK, the Big Thank You,* and *the Big Wow.*

The first, the Big OK, is acceptance of the world as it is. We can make all effort for a better one, and should, but we must also not deny that it is as it is. We must come to terms with the flaws, the suffering, the injustice, even as we seek to improve them.

The second, the Big Thank You, is the lesson of gratitude. From scalp to soles, it is an abiding thankfulness and welcoming for the tremendous gift that is this life and its experiences.

Finally: the Big Wow, which is frankly just looking around and paying attention to this magnificent Universe. It's all so amazing, so fantastic, so beautiful. Down to the tiniest scales and up to the largest, appreciating where we are can lead to nothing less than Wow.

Humanity faces many challenges. We have a global climate crisis, crashing biodiversity, and the threat of authoritarianism and stripping away or denial of basic human rights. Simply reading the daily news can be a real challenge to our mental health and well-being.

All of this is true. Anyone paying attention struggles with it.

I certainly struggle with it.

And yet: look out the window.

Above, the short-wavelength light scatters through the atmosphere to create a blue vault dancing with white, ever-changing clouds, bringing the rain that is life.

Below, the green things, breathing our waste carbon and turning the light of the Sun into the sugar that will feed, eventually, everything on Earth.

Flitting birds: adventurers across thousands of miles of arduous migration as a simple routine of their lives. The many forms of miraculous life.

The good, good Earth.

We have come so far, you and I, from the ocean depths to land, to the land mass that became Africa, stepping down from trees to the ground, brains growing, making tools, and on, dreaming, and on, imagining, and out, until our very dreams brought us to the Moon, our machines far out into space.

We are the most amazing marvels we are aware of, anywhere in the Universe.

Do not forget the glory. Do not forget the wonder.

Do not forget the generous blessing of the air that fills our lungs with each breath. Nor the magic of the cycles of water than keep us alive. The magnetosphere and ionosphere that shield us from harsh radiation, sheltering a balmy, temperate little bubble within which we can live.

Yes, these times are hard. That is true.

But this is ***life:*** the Big Show! The Great Adventure! A precious, too-brief one-way tour through the spectacular glories of the world.

And we are here in a time when we can see so much, can learn so much about this amazing phenomenon of which we are a part: the Universe.

Too soon, we are folded back into the fabric of nature.

Look for the wonder, folks. Seize the joy. Don't forget that they are always there, even now.

### *Meditation on the Three Big Lessons*

Seriously take time to contemplate the Three Big Lessons: the Big OK, the Big Thanks, and the Big Wow. See where you have a hard time accepting one or more of them, and work on that. Just getting these three understandings firmly under your belt will make a huge difference in your life experience. Here is a simple ritual you can do to assist.

#### PREPARATION

Place three unlit candles in holders before you. Get something delicious to eat or drink and have it standing by.

#### ARRIVAL

Ground (see "Arrival" under "Ritual Basics")

#### WORKING AND GRATITUDE

Light the first candle. Say, "This is the world. It is filled with beauty. This is the world. It is filled with horror. This is the world, and I accept that this is the world. I say, 'Okay'. May the world be seen and honored."

Light the second candle. Say, "This is the world, generous beyond measure. This is the world, warm and sweet and nourishing. This is the world, where love dwells, and I say, 'Thanks' I am grateful for my many gifts."

Light the third candle. Say, "This is the magnificent world, astounding in its wonders. This is the sky, filled with jewels and fire. This is the miracle that I am here, given this sweet life. This is the world, and I say 'Wow!'"

#### BENEDICTION

Say, "With this celebration, I honor reality. I acknowledge it, I am grateful for it, and I am amazed by it. May the deliciousness of this (food or drink) nourish and delight me, as does the world." Eat or drink the delicious thing you have brought. When it is gone, blow out the candles; the ritual is over.

## Engaging with the Earth

As you settle into a regular seasonal ritual practice, you will find that you are more attuned to the changing of the seasons, more aware of what is happening in nature in your area. You will probably always have a good sense of where the Moon is in its cycle, for example. Here are two techniques you can use to further this process, to build a deeper sense of connection and reverence with the Earth of which we are a part: *ritual pilgrimage* and *creating a sacred landscape through myth-making.*

### *Ritual Pilgrimage*

In a ritual pilgrimage, you make a trip to a beloved nature spot, a museum or other destination into a spiritual activity by assigning an overlay of meaning onto the simple process of hiking or traveling. You can add a symbolic, ritual dimension to a hike in nature or a voyage to a special exhibit in a museum, or some other meaningful destination: turning a day trip into a *pilgrimage* to a special place with meaning and significance. Here is a step-by-step guide to creating such a pilgrimage for yourself:

- **Identify a destination** for your hike: a spring, a pool, a waterfall, a rock formation, a particular stand of trees, a mountaintop, a spectacular overlook, a particular exhibit in a museum.
- **Decide what that destination stands for** (a theme or intention for the ritual), and name it: "The Fountain of Good Fortune"; "The Glade of Restoration"; "The Pillar of the Ancestors." It is to this destination that your pilgrimage will proceed.
- **Bring a libation** to pour, or other (completely natural, aesthetically-pleasing) offerings. Be aware of the potential impact of any food items on wildlife: non-toxic flowers, nuts and thin-skinned fruits are generally okay; bread and citrus fruit are not.
- At the outset of your travel to the site, **prepare yourself** by observing a moment of silence and contemplating the goal of your pilgrimage. Any special practices you prefer for centering and calming your mind are appropriate here.
- As you travel, **identify "special places"** along the way—a large tree or one with a hole in it, for example, or a rock outcropping, or a spring: anywhere that seems special—**where you will pour a libation or leave a little offering.** Make each offering "in the name of" a quality or emotion with which you wish to imbue

your pilgrimage or a commitment you make in the name of securing the blessings of the destination.

- **At your destination,** set out symbolic items to create an impromptu Focus (this may not be possible in a public venue like a museum). Make your final offering and speak your wishes at having completed your pilgrimage. You may want to stay and eat a snack at the destination, to "share a meal" with the essence of the place. If it's a water source, you may want to gather a little water in a bottle and keep it for usage in rituals later.
- **Thank the place for its blessings** before you go, pack up your Focus and leave the destination looking as you found it (save, perhaps, for a small, biodegradable offering if it is a natural area—nuts and soft-skinned fruits like a few grapes are good choices).

Pilgrimage hiking can help us to "overlay" a sacred, metaphorical landscape of symbolic meaning over the physical landscapes of the natural places we love. Over time, your landscape can come to be filled with special places that have particular meanings. Perhaps, as discussed in the following section, you can develop myth stories to explain why these places are associated with these meanings.

In any case, it's a way to enjoy our sojourns in a different, intentional way.

## Imagining a Mythic Landscape through Storytelling

Throughout human history, cultures have communicated their values and moral codes through storytelling. Both oral traditions and literate societies passed their teaching stories from generation to generation. These stories illustrated the values of their cultures, gave explanations for how they had come to exist as distinct groups, and often populated the home landscapes of these cultures with mythological beings and powers.

As a whole, such stories had the effect not only of passing along the beliefs of their peoples, but of *filling their landscapes with narratives of enchantment and magic.* Major features of the lands where these people lived—rivers, mountains, geological features—became associated with stories of heroism, discovery, innovation, magic, and lessons learned.

Where I live—North America—the vast majority of the residents have never lived in an enchanted landscape, because we are colonizers. Our myths are of far-off places we or our cultural traditions came from, like Palestine, or England, Ireland, Italy, or Greece. Only the Indigenous peoples have stories that are about *this* land, and we are generally not privy to them unless we are one of them. Nor would it be appropriate to steal their stories for our own.

### *Create Your Own Myth*

I suggest we create our own stories, either by ourselves or in concert with others we share our Earth-honoring rituals with.

Here's an example.

Some years ago, I wrote a series of stories about Sonoma County, where I live. I begin my stories with "What if?" because they are speculative, imagined histories. They are meant for enjoyment and for illustration of their moral lessons, not to be literal instruction about the nature of the world.

I think that as we develop relationships with our local landscapes, it is natural that such stories would occur to us. They're useful for teaching lessons to children, and they imbue the features of our local terrain with a mythic sacredness that might otherwise not be as deeply felt or communicated.

Here is one of the sacred landscape stories I have written for my region, Sonoma County in California:

RACCOON MAKES CANDY

What if this happened, a long time ago, before the Human People came here?

*It was just when everything was beginning. Across the land of Sonoma, everything was there just for the first time. There were Eagle, and Fox, and Salmon and Elk and Hummingbird, and all the other Animal People and Plant People, but there was only one of each. They had sprung up in Sonoma's footsteps as she stepped out of the sea, and each was different.*

*It was beautiful, in the wide valleys along the River, and the People were all happy. Some flew, others swam. They found places to live: in holes, in trees, in pools. No one ate anything.*

*But after a while, it was boring and lonely. The Animal People and the Plant People thought, what is this? What must I do? Is this all there is, just to sit around in all this beauty all day?*

*Raccoon was there, too. He climbed up onto Mt. St. Helens and looked down. He could see that Unhappiness was being invented. Being Raccoon, he wasn't bored yet, but he could see how it might happen. And he had an idea.*

*He called Bear, and Valley Oak, and Salmon, and they all came to where he sat on the mountaintop. He had scooped a hollow in the rock up there, and the bare stone was getting hot in the midday sun.*

*"Friends," said Raccoon, "I am making something. I need you to bring me what I need, and then I will share it with all of you."*

*"What is it?" asked Salmon.*

*"I am making candy," said Raccoon.*

*"What is that!?" said the Animal People and Oak.*

*"You put it in your mouth and it makes you feel very good," said Raccoon. "That is called eating."*

*Well, this was the first new thing that had happened in a long time, and all the People were excited. They said they would help Raccoon make the candy.*

*So Raccoon sent Bear to find honey, and asked Valley Oak for acorns, and sent Salmon to a clear pool in the River, where she brought back a flashing reflection from the water.*

*When they brought back these things, Raccoon ground the acorns, and put them into the warm hollow in the mountaintop. Then he crushed in the honeycombs, and the flash of Sun, and stirred these all together.*

*"Now go down the mountain, and don't come back until the Moon has risen," said Raccoon.*

*When they were gone, Raccoon invited another Animal Person to help him. Black Widow Spider was living in a crack on top of Mt. St. Helena, and still lives there to this day. "Grandmother," said Raccoon, "will you hlp me to make this candy?"*

*So Grandmother Spider came out and added what she had to the hollow in the mountaintop. And Raccoon put in the shining reflection that Salmon had brought back from the River, and covered the candy up.*

*"Now we wait," he said.*

*Soon the Moon rose. Word had gone around about Raccoon's wonderful idea, so when the Moon rose, all the Animal People and Plant People came there, up to the top of Mt. St. Helena in the silver light. They all wanted to see what this candy was going to be like.*

*Raccoon stood on top of a rock, and he looked out in the Moonlight at all the People gathered there.*

*"Friends, this is a special candy. It is very sweet, but it will be bitter, too. When you come to the hollow for a taste, first look at the candy, and I will show you what to do."*

*So Squirrel, who is always in a hurry, stepped up to the hollow, and took away the cover. In the moonlight, the surface of the candy was black and shining. Squirrel could see an exact copy of herself reflected there ... and then the copy stepped up out of the hollow to stand next to her! Now there were two squirrels.*

*They weren't exactly the same, either.*

*Raccoon took some of the candy and rubbed it on the parts of the two Squirrels that were different from each other. "This will make these parts sweet. So now you don't have to be alone, and you can make more Squirrels. We will have children now, and fill the world with our families."*

*The Animal People and the Plant People crowded around, excited, and they all brought their mates out of the candy and rubbed their new genitals with it. This was wonderful! No more loneliness!*

*The Moon had almost set when the last of them went back down the mountain, happy with a new mate.*

*Then Black Widow Spider came out again. She said, "You didn't tell them about the other part."*

*"Yeah," said Raccoon. "We needed to get things going around here, and I was afraid they wouldn't take the candy if I told them."*

*"If they had thought about it a little, they would have known. It wouldn't have taken long to fill up the whole world." Spider shifted a little and sighed, and walked over to where the last of the candy lay glimmering in the hollow. She leaned over the edge to see her lover's face, and when he had climbed, with his handsome shining new legs, to stand beside her, she solemnly rubbed their genitals with the sweetness and bitterness of love and death.*

## Engaging with Your Village, Town, City, or Society

Finding meaning in life isn't just about paying attention and finding the golden moments. It's also about what you do: what you stand for, what your presence in the world helps to create.

Nearly every community has needs: people who need help, environmental problems. Being aware of these problems and helping to solve them is another approach to creating meaning in our lives, a legacy to persist long after we are dead. As the 8th Atheopagan Principle, Legacy, states: we have a responsibility to the future. Or, as the American poet Wendell Berry said, "The world is not given from (our) fathers but borrowed from our children."[12]

One way you can contribute to the future of your community and the world is to become active in causes that matter to you. Most decision-making in a democracy boils down to local politics, as who gets elected to make decisions is a local matter. By working to elect people who generally share your values and vision for the future, and by advocating to those currently in office to push for better policies, we can make a real difference, and can also build community by finding like-minded people to organize and advocate with.

12. Wendell Berry, *The Unforeseen Wilderness: An Essay on Kentucky's Red River Gorge* (Lexington, KT: The University Press of Kentucky), 1971.

There are, of course, many opportunities to volunteer in our communities which are not directly linked to policy decisions. Organizations of every stripe need help in providing their services to the needy, in planting and maintaining habitat restoration projects, and in delivering educational and artistic services to the public. Find something that feels meaningful to you and get involved! You will find that your life feels even richer if you are not only celebrating golden moments but giving back.

In any case, it matters in living a meaningful life that we stand for something other than just our own interests and wishes. It's a bit trite, but it really does feel better to give than to receive when it comes to what we live our lives for.

Conclusion

# Welcome to the Journey!

Well, having arrived here, you have completed the first steps in your evolution toward better, happier, more effective living. By implementing the techniques outlined in this book, you have begun rewarding practices that will serve you for the rest of your life.

As these observances and celebrations and personal rituals start to be the "new normal" for you, you may find yourself feeling more of an impulse to cultivate new experiences and adventures. Listen to that impulse, and make sure you aren't living your entire life between the rails of what people expect of you or what you think is "normal" for yourself. Life is short, and it can be amazing!

If, through the course of reading, you find yourself resonating with the Atheopagan values and worldview, we welcome you to join our communities online. We have a Facebook group at facebook.com/groups/Atheopaganism, and a Discord server you can find by searching Discord for "Atheopaganism" and requesting an invitation. You may also enjoy our podcast, "The Wonder: Science-Based Paganism" and/or our YouTube channel, each of which releases new episodes weekly.

In any case, give yourself some real credit and appreciation for making a decision to upgrade your life! I hope you have enjoyed the journey thus far.

May the Sacred Earth and Cosmos inspire and delight you as you experience the marvelous, brief gift that is your life. My very best and fondest wishes to you and to those you will bring along with you.

I will leave you with this poem, which I wrote in a moment of sublime joy after a ritual.

May you enjoy many such moments.

**ECSTASY**

Ever more open; arms flung wide
Let the warm, wet wings of your chest be spread until
Barehearted there
Only the longing of joy is with you,
The sweetness of Life's unfolding generosity.
They are all there, the great and tiny miracles daily given,
A breath, a golden pebble, a scarlet cloud at sunset,
The voice of the Cosmos, singing out to cold space,
Out to blackness and beginnings all
Whirling and singing and spinning
Sacred
Ever-changing
The glory of the world in your heart's red petals there
Where first it placed a red kiss in your mother's womb
Saying Welcome.

# Part 3
# Resources

# Seasonal Crafts

These are the craft projects listed in the section on celebrating the holidays of the Wheel of the Year. Some of them may be useful at other times of the year as well, or just for fun. Working on an art or craft project is a great way to access the ritual state of mind: with high concentration, focus on the present and the glow that comes from being a creator.

## Midwinter: Log Ritual

We have many traditions drawn forth from antiquity for the Midwinter time of year: the burning of candles and colorful lights, the decoration of the home with evergreen boughs and holly and other plants which persist in life through the dark months, and, of course, the "Christmas" tree, a Pagan holdover into modern times.

One such old tradition is the Yule or Midwinter Log. While found in various forms, here is what I have adapted as a tradition for my household's celebrations.

### *Materials*

2 ft (.65 m) of the trunk of the previous year's Midwinter tree

A split oaken log

Cotton, sisal, or other natural twine

Decorations: boughs of holly and/or pyracantha with plenty of red berries if possible; coniferous trees preferably with cones

White flour

### *Instructions*

Use twine to bind the Midwinter tree log tightly to the split oak log

Tuck decorations under the twine until it is festive and attractive; use more twine if necessary

A dusting of flour will create a snow effect

If you don't have a fireplace or fire pit, drill holes so that taper candles can be inserted in the log, allowing the log to be "burned" by lighting the candles and letting them burn down. Be sure to put the log on a fireproof surface.

### *Ritual*

On Midwinter night, contemplate the coming year, and write wishes for the coming year on slips of paper. Tuck these under the twine and boughs.

On the night of the solstice, make hot beverages, and sit outside with loved ones in the cold and dark for a while, to feel the character of the season. Then light a single taper each and return inside, where all lights have been extinguished except the Midwinter tree. Light candles which have been placed throughout the house, to bring the light back.

Then, gently carry the log to your fireplace or fire pit (or the place where you will burn the candles). Sing a seasonal song and light the log (or candles) ablaze.

The Midwinter log is a fun project to do, and the entire family can help with making and creating it. Just be sure that everything on it is plastic-free, to avoid creating toxic fumes.

## The Brightening: Homemade Incense

Incense is a powerful tool in ritual, which explains why religions all over the world use it. Scent can lead us off into memory or evoke a sudden sense of sacredness and magic. Certain incenses like frankincense have been scientifically proved to improve mood.[13] Since the Brightening is a time of year often associated with preparation of tools and plans for future work, it's a good time to lay in a stock of homemade incenses. Here's a little primer on making incense generally, with a recipe for a nice early-spring blend.

These are directions for making loose incense, which is burned on a charcoal tablet or thrown on a fire. You will need a mortar and pestle—preferably one with a heavy mortar so it isn't tippy.

### *Ingredients*

There are four general categories of materials which can go into incense. Here they are, in the order they should be added to your mixture:

- Liquids (like essential oils—use tiny amounts) and resins such as frankincense, pine pitch, myrrh, and dragon's blood
- Woody ingredients such as fir, pine, sandalwood, apple wood, bark, and dried berries such as juniper
- Powdered ingredients such as spices and herbs
- Fresh ingredients such as herbs and aromatic flowers

Depending on the quantity of each incense you want to create, you may need to repeat the creation process several times to complete your batch. I recommend small batches to start with, so you can experiment with the scent.

You usually want to have the bulk of your incense made up of something that will stay burning and keep the mixture alight, like pinewood or sandalwood or pine needles. That said, if you plan to refresh the incense regularly and have a solidly glowing charcoal tablet to place it on, you can have more of your mixture made up of other materials.

13. Federation of American Societies for Experimental Biology. "Burning incense is psychoactive: New class of antidepressants might be right under our noses." ScienceDaily. ScienceDaily, 20 May 2008.

What scents you choose are up to you, of course, but more floral or citrus scents tend to be associated with springtime, spicy scents with summer, the scent of burning hardwood leaves with autumn, and resinous incenses such as frankincense, myrrh and dragon's blood with winter. Earthy scents such as cedar and yew are associated with mourning. Look around: there are plenty of recipes available on the Internet.

### *Instructions*

Crush your ingredients, adding them one at a time, in the order previously described, to your mortar and pestle until you have formed a paste or powder containing all the ingredients. This is important so ingredients are mixed thoroughly and will burn in the proportions you have chosen.

One warning: some plants and substances (like camphor and cinnamon) can be toxic when burned and, if used at all, should be used in small proportions. Confirm that the ingredients you want to combine into an incense are safe to burn before including them. Some incenses can also trigger allergies or asthma in those who suffer from them, so always seek consent from people with you before lighting incense.

### *Early Spring Blend*

For a nice early-spring incense blend, I recommend:

2 parts dry cedar

2 parts frankincense

1 part pine resin

½ part dried lemon peel

½ part dried orange peel

½ part dried rose petals

¼ part clove

When you have completed preparing your seasonal incense, you may want to speak an intention over it to "bless" it to the purpose you want for it to mean. Store all incenses in airtight jars to conserve their freshness.

## The Brightening: Dream Sachet

The scent of mugwort is said to bring wise and vivid dreams. Whether or not this is true, it is a pleasant scent to go to sleep to.

### *Materials*

About an ounce of dried mugwort, which you can often gather wild (it's rather invasive in many areas) and dry by hanging in bundles upside down, in a low oven or in a food dehydrator. When the mugwort is dry, remove stems and chop the leaves finely.

A piece of sheet-weight cotton fabric about 4 in on a side

### *Instructions*

Sew the fabric into a two-inch by four-inch bag, preferably by hand and in ritual space. Play dreamy music while you are doing this to invoke dreaming and dreams.

When the bag is complete, turn it inside out so the raw edges of the fabric are hidden inside, then stuff the bag with the mugwort. Sew the fourth side of the bag shut, sealing the mugwort in.

Optionally, you can include a slip of paper with a sigil (see page 84 for sigil creation) for good dreams in the sachet.

Slip the sachet inside your pillow at night and enjoy!

## High Spring: Naturally Dyed, Leaf-Printed Eggs

Dyeing and painting eggs is a European spring tradition going back many centuries. In Ukraine, painstakingly wax-resistance dyed eggs known as *pysanky* are magnificent art objects, typically bearing springtime symbols like birds and new green shoots. Early spring is when many birds lay their eggs in Europe, and eggs were the first fresh protein source available in the wild after the long winter, so eggs have become associated with springtime, as in the Christian Easter, which of course has nothing to do with eggs (or rabbits).

These are instructions for making beautifully dyed eggs for spring celebrations, using natural dyes and printing them with attractive leaf patterns.

They look beautiful on a spring Focus or a High Spring feast's table centerpiece, and can, of course, be eaten afterward.

## *Materials*

Natural dyeing agents (red cabbage, turmeric, onion skins, beets, mint and coffee)

Eggs, hard-boiled and cooled (or raw, if you want to blow and keep them after dying)

White vinegar

Large cooking pot

Bowls for dye solutions, one for each color you make

Tongs

Paper towels

Nylon stockings or silk fabric

Fresh leaves

## *Instructions*

Make the dyes:

In a two-quart pot, to each of these (one at a time) add one quart of water and two teaspoons white vinegar, boil, and simmer for thirty-five minutes. Strain each dye into a separate bowl you will use for dying the eggs.

| | |
|---|---|
| Brown | Strong black coffee (no vinegar needed) |
| Blue | 4 cups shredded red cabbage |
| Yellow/gold | 3 tsp turmeric |
| Green | 4 cups fresh mint, chopped (heat but do not boil) |
| Orange | 4 cups yellow onion skins, chopped |

### DRESS THE EGGS IN LEAF WRAPPINGS

Cut nylon stockings or silk into small bands, approximately five inches long, one for each egg you will dye.

Make sure eggs are dry. Then place a fresh leaf onto each egg and press lightly, so that the dye does not get underneath the leaves.

Wrap gently but snugly in the nylon or silk and tie closed with a knot or rubber band on both ends. The tighter you can get the wrapping the better but be careful not to crack the egg.

DYE THE EGGS

**Light Blue:** Soak eggs in room-temperature cabbage solution, thirty minutes.

**Dark Blue:** Soak eggs in room-temperature cabbage solution overnight.

**Light Green:** Soak eggs in room-temperature mint solution thirty minutes.

**Dark Green:** Soak eggs in room-temperature mint solution overnight.

**Pale Yellow:** Soak eggs in room-temperature turmeric solution, thirty minutes.

**Orange:** Soak eggs in room-temperature onion-skin solution, thirty minutes.

**Light Brown:** Soak eggs in room-temperature black coffee, thirty minutes.

**Dark Brown:** Soak eggs in room-temperature black coffee overnight.

**Light Pink:** Soak eggs in room-temperature beet solution, thirty minutes.

Remove stockings and leaves from eggs.

Dab off excess dye with a paper towel and leave to dry for several hours

When dry, cut nylon open and gently peel off leaves. What will result are beautifully dyed eggs with the pattern of leaves printed on them.

## May Day: Flower Crown

A lovely spring crown of bright flowers is traditional in springtime or for May Day in many places in Europe. You can't help but feel festive and light-hearted when wearing one.

### *Materials*

Florists' wire (or pipe cleaners twisted together end to end to make a length long enough to go around your head; preferably green). Alternatively, ivy or grape vines can be used to make the main body of the crown.

Spring flowers, such as irises, daisies, petunias, roses, and wildflowers (leave the stems on but remove any thorns)

Ribbon in festive bright colors

### *Instructions*

Take wire (or ivy, or grape vine) and create a circle that will fit your head. Weave or tie the ends together firmly to form the body of the crown.

Next, take more wire (or ivy, etc.) and twist it around the ring, creating a framework for you to add your flowers.

Weave the stems of the flowers through the frame. Tuck the flowers in right up against one another so that the frame is covered. If you have trouble getting them to stay in place, or if they seem loose, wrap a bit more florist's wire around them for additional stability. You can also use florist's green tape to wrap around the stems and wire framework to bind it all in place.

Finally, cut ribbons to varied lengths. Tie them to the back of the wreath so they drape down your back. Put on your crown, and you're ready to go dance around the Maypole!

## May Day: Maypole

Dancing the Maypole is a tradition from across Europe and many centuries old. While traditions vary, the Maypole and dance here are a simple and generic form of this very old ritual.

To do a Maypole dance, you will need a location that is level, preferably grass or comfortably springy soil, and available for digging a hole. The area you need depends on the number of dancers you hope to accommodate, but it should be at least thirty feet across to accommodate dancers, musicians and those watching but not dancing.

### *Materials*

A pole at least nine feet long and five inches to seven inches in diameter. A section of surplused telephone or power pole is perfect. The dimensions are important: you need to embed about eighteen inches of the pole in the ground in order for it to be stable during the Maypole dance, and a pole of any narrower diameter will take forever for the ribbons to be wrapped on the pole. Think about it: if every turn around the pole is only taking up a few inches of ribbon, you'll be going around that pole for a long, long time before you've used up the long ribbons you're dancing with.

- A flower crown for the Maypole made out of baling wire. This crown goes over the top of the pole and is held firmly in place there and is decorated with flowers (florists' wire is helpful for affixing the flowers to the wire structure; decorating the flower crown is often a group activity before the Maypole dance)-.
- Ribbons—one for each dancer, about fifteen feet to twenty feet long—are tied onto the flower crown at the hub (next to the pole).

### *Instructions*

Affix the flower crown to the pole and then dig an eighteen-inch to two-foot deep hole to receive the pole. Carefully tilt up the pole and put the opposite end from the flower crown in the ground, packing dirt all around it until it is firmly seated. A posthole digger helps for this part.

Now you should have your Maypole! With ribbons dangling down from the flower crown, and ready to be danced and wrapped up.

## *The Maypole Dance*

This is a very simple, country-style dance. Dancers are designated into two groups, each group established by alternating every other dancer standing in the circle around the pole ("A, B, A, B" etc.). The "A"s go clockwise around the pole; the "B"s go counterclockwise, so dancers start out in pairs facing one another, holding their ribbons. As they begin to go around the pole, when dancers pass each other, they raise and lower the hand holding the ribbon rhythmically to guide the ribbon over and then under the dancers they encounter, creating an "over… under… over… under" pattern that weaves the ribbons on the pole. As you dance, make eye contact with the dancers coming toward you, and smile!

There is quite a bit of traditional British music that is associated with dancing the Maypole. Live musicians are best, but barring that, I quite like the music of the New England ensemble Bare Necessities, from their album *Take a Dance.*

It is inevitable that while dancing the Maypole, there will be mistakes, and that is a part of the charm. This is a fun and joyous ritual activity, not an exercise in precision.

When the ribbons are mostly woven on the pole and there are only short ends left, blow a whistle, or ring a bell to signal that everyone should now go clockwise and simply race around the pole with their ribbons, no longer going over and under. This will wind the ends of the ribbons about the pole and complete the Maypole dance.

All of the elements of the Maypole ritual can be augmented with additional ritual components. I have attended Maypole rituals where men carried in the pole and anointed it with oil, for example, and women constructed the flower crown and dug the hole. Some consider this exclusionary of genderfluid and nonbinary folks, however, so be sure you're thinking through your choices in light of the group you will be working with.

In any event, experiment and make the Maypole ritual your own! While this is a tradition that goes back at least to the Middle Ages in Germanic and Scandinavian countries, it is a living tradition, and you should feel free to put your own stamp on it.

## May Day: Consensual Pomander Ball Game

This is a sexy, flirty game for adults about communication and boundaries. The Pomander Orange is a small orange which has been studded all over with cloves. This is an age-old tradition; these were used by nobles in some countries to help mask the many unpleasant odors of life in the Middle Ages and Renaissance. For some of these elites, oranges themselves were rare and exotic imports from faraway places, and not simply fruit to be eaten.

### *Materials*

One small orange

Cloves

### *Instructions*

Stud the orange all over with cloves

### *Game Rules*

The Pomander Orange game can take place as a formal activity, but it can also be fun to have the Orange going around while other activities are taking place, such as at a party.

Our rules for the Orange are as follows:

1. No one has to participate in the game if they don't want to. Some signal or marker will be provided to designate people who aren't playing. Depending on the group and circumstances, other rules (such as an above-the-waist rule) may be applied.
2. The holder of the Orange may approach any person who is participating at the game. They take a clove from the Orange, give it to the approachee, and propose a type of interaction in the

form of a request for permission. Kissing is the most common interaction requested.

3. The approachee may agree or disagree with the request or may make a counterproposal. *Both participants must agree on what they are going to do before they do it.* "No, thank you," is a perfectly acceptable answer to any proposal.
4. The two participants carry out the agreed-upon interaction.
5. After the interaction, the person who was approached now holds the Pomander Orange, and the process repeats, with that person selecting another person to approach.
6. The game ends when the Orange has no more cloves, or at the end of a designated period of time.

It can look like this. Sarah, having received the Orange, approaches Sam, giving him a clove from the Orange and asking, "May I kiss you?" Sam replies, "Yes, but no tongues, please." (Alternatively, he could just say yes or no to the proposal, or he could say that he would not like to be kissed but would exchange a hug with her). They kiss, Sam takes the Orange, and he begins to look around for another participant to approach.

Note that this game is not only about flirting, sexy interaction and boundaries, but also about *clarity of communication*: having the courage to ask unequivocally for what you want.

Also, given concerns about communicable diseases, if you're going to hold an event where this game is played, be sure everyone attending understands that they must not play if they have any reason to believe they may be ill.

## Midsummer: Sun Broom

Crafted on the longest day of the year, the Sun broom is both a Midsummer ritual and a tool you can use ritually around the year. The Sun broom is a great tool for drawing a circle to create sacred space at the beginning of the Midsummer ritual, too ... or any time it feels like the Sun's power would be welcome. The Sun broom is a prominent part of my Midsummer ritual Focus, as well.

This is a ritual I like to repeat in the dead of winter. When things start feeling really gray and cold, it feels good to trot out the Sun broom and give the house a once-over, remembering summer and warmth. And you can always use it if things around the house are feeling icky and need some of that cleansing, illuminating sunshine.

### *Materials*

A piece of tree branch about two to three inches long for the broom handle. Don't hurt a tree; go for a hike and find something that has already fallen to the ground.

Thin ribbon or strong twine for binding grasses to the handle.

A bunch of long strands of dry grass. I harvest the grass at the height of the day on Midsummer—the peak of the power of the Sun in the Northern Hemisphere. In my particular area, wild oats grow very tall, so I use those, mostly.

### *Instructions*

Bind the grass to the handle with the ribbon, singing *we all come from the infinite Sun, forever and ever and ever.*

Be certain to bind the grasses tightly to the handle—they may look dry but will dry out further and shrink. Otherwise the grass bundle could fly off the handle in mid-use, which undermines the solemnity of the enterprise.

Once constructed, I leave the broom to sit in the Sun until sunset on Midsummer, "charging" in the high summer Sun.

### *Ritual*

The next day, use your Sun broom to virtually "sweep" your home, moving from room to room and sweeping the air to bring light and warmth to every corner. You might sing (or hum) "Here Comes the Sun" or "I Can See Clearly Now" while doing so.

The next year, refresh your Sun broom by unwrapping the bindings and letting last year's grasses go back into the Earth, then cut a new bundle of grasses and rebind your broom.

Enjoy your Sun broom, and may it bring you a sense of strength and power and warming light throughout the year!

## The Dimming: Ritual Mask

Masks have been used for ritual purposes for thousands of years. The oldest known mask is made of stone and was found in Asia Minor; it is 9,000 years old.[14] Far older depictions of what appear to be men wearing masks are found in Paleolithic cave paintings dating to 30,000–40,000 years ago. Ritual masks, therefore, are a time-honored and powerful tradition. Let's make one!

### *Setting Up*

I recommend that you *make your mask in ritual space.* Center yourself, light candles, burn incense and do whatever else you need to do to achieve the shift into ritual state (however, be sure you have sufficient lighting to see what you are doing). A ritual mask is a work of intentionality, and everything about how it is created and handled from its very inception should be done mindfully and with respect for its meaning and purpose.

There are a couple of directions you can go with developing mask tools for ritual. One is to create a single mask that is your tool for all rituals; in that case, you will want the design not to be too specifically themed on any one particular quality or personality. Alternatively, you can create multiple masks for different qualities and personalities and select from them when planning a ritual which requires a particular character.

There are advantages to each approach. In the former case, the ritual mask becomes a tool you will come to associate with accumulated years of ritual observances—an association that will steadily increase the sense of power and gravitas felt when putting it on. In the latter, specialized masks

14. Williams, A. R., "World's Oldest Masks Modeled on Early Farmers' Ancestors" (National Geographic), 2014

can be developed which communicate the characteristics you embody when wearing them, allowing more "targeted focus" on those particular qualities represented by a particular mask.

In any event, whether you stop with just one or develop a collection, it all starts with the first. So let's get started.

Spend some time thinking about your design. Think about what *your* ritual and observational life feels like, and the emotional tone you want to communicate with the mask. Do sketches and search online to look at the wide range of masks that are out there: Carnivale masks, Indigenous masks, etc. Remember: this is a powerful ritual tool, and you want it to provoke a feeling of fascination and riveted attention when your fellow celebrants see you wearing it. *Don't copy Indigenous designs*—that's cultural appropriation, and not cool—but you can be inspired by them to create your own design.

I prefer to use a half-mask that leaves the lower part of the face exposed. This maintains a humanity about the mask that is otherwise lost if the entire face is covered, requiring fellow celebrants to relate to a stiff and unmoving "face" (usually with a muffled voice, too). While there are sometimes when an alien, inhuman face may be the most effective for use in a given ritual, I find that in most cases the half-mask feels more appropriate and enables me to project the personality of the mask I am wearing/carrying more effectively. Another, quite dramatic option is to shape the mask in a "Phantom of the Opera" style, leaving nearly half of the face exposed.

Now, for a base armature, you can start with a commercial mask base. But I think it's better to mold the base mask to your own face so it is really, *really* personal. Instructions for making your own papier-mâché mask follow: it's easy.

### *Materials*

Mirror

Newspaper, cut into strips (¾ in width is perfect)

Large kitchen bowl

All-purpose flour

Scissors

Petroleum jelly, or olive oil

Fan for drying the mask once formed

Decorative supplies (paint, sequins, beads, natural objects, etc.)

Hot glue gun

A custom-made papier-mâché mask fits well and feels comfortable because you use your own face as a mold. Paper-mache does, however, take time to dry. Make your mask at least twenty-four hours before you want to use it.

### *Instructions*

Mix flour paste. In the bowl, mix together one part flour and three parts water until smooth. Add a little more water or flour to adjust the thickness of the paste as you wish.

Prepare for the mask. Set up a comfortable, well-lit spot in front of the mirror. Place the paste and newspaper strips nearby. Apply a protective layer of petroleum jelly to your face, brows, and hairline. If you are allergic to petroleum, try using olive oil.

Dip two strips of newspaper into the paste, coating both sides. Place one strip diagonally from the lower left nostril across the bridge of the nose and ending over the right brow. Smooth flat. Lay the second strip diagonally in the opposite direction, ending over the left brow and forming an "X." This helps provide a firm structure to build on for the rest of the mask.

Move to the forehead. Dip a strip of newspaper into the paste. Apply it horizontally across the forehead. Smooth flat. Work around each side of the forehead, applying more newspaper strips. Overlap about half of the previous newspaper strip with each new one.

Wrap the eye sockets and nose. Continue wrapping newspaper strips from the temples around the eyes. Leave the eyes open -- you will need to see while you work. Wrap the newspaper strips around the bottom of the eye sockets and over the nose. A last strip over the nose will secure both sides of the face together. If you are making a half-mask, stop here and let the newspaper dry.

Finish the lower half of the face (if your mask is to have one). Outline the rest of the face, lower jaw, and chin with newspaper strips. Work inward from the outside, overlapping strips as you go. If you want to leave a mouth hole, work around the mouth in the same manner used to wrap around the eyes.

Add another layer to the mask. For a thicker, more durable paper mask, repeat steps four through six.

Allow the mask to set. Set up a small room fan nearby. Sit back and relax for about an hour while the mask sets. The air from the fan helps some of the excess water to evaporate.

Remove the mask. Lean forward, holding your hands against the mask. Gently "scrunch" and move the muscles of your face to work the mask loose. Ease the mask away from your face. It will still be mostly wet at this point, so be very careful.

Set the mask in front of the fan to help it completely dry out. It can take up to twenty-four hours for the paper to dry entirely. You can also dry a mask in an oven set on extremely low heat (100° F) for an hour or so.

Now decorate the mask (see following section).

### *Tips for Success*

It can help to have a friend put the strips on your face. This is a good idea for a full face mold. Use a short straw between your lips to breathe through if creating a full face mold.

You can add papier-mâché extensions (claws, tentacles, the Sun's rays, etc.) to expand your mask out from your face.

I like to glue a layer of muslin cut to the shape of the mask on the inside, to protect the papier-mâché from being softened by sweat and my face from getting dusty white when I wear the mask. Another alternative is to coat the back of the mask with clear lacquer. Be sure it has completely dried before putting the mask on, as fumes can burn the eyes.

Now comes the fun part: to decorate it.

### *Decorating Your Mask*

Start with a base coat of paint to establish the overall color. Then you can add painted designs, sequins, beads, feathers, buttons, bones, shells or any other decorative items using a hot glue gun. Colored fabric glue can be used to established raised lines or beads. Coat with clear lacquer when finished, to protect your design (again, be sure it is *completely dry* before wearing, as paint or lacquer fumes can burn the eyes).

When your mask is ready, consecrate it with a ritual intended to give it meaning and power to you. You may want to keep it on your Focus, pass it through incense smoke or sprinkle it with water you have sat out in the light of the Moon, invoke qualities you hope to embody with the mask, or otherwise perform ritual actions that reinforce to your subconscious mind the importance and specialness of the mask. It is essential that you are able to suspend disbelief and *be* what the mask represents in order for others also to see you this way.

Keep your ritual mask on your Focus or somewhere else where it will be respected, such as hung on the wall in a special place in your home. Always remember: this is/will be The Face of the Ineffable for your fellow ritual celebrants. It should always be treated with reverence—doing so will increase its effectiveness in facilitating ritual transformation both for you and for fellow celebrants.

## Harvest: Corn Dolly

Sometimes this craft project is linked with the Brightening, given its association with infancy, but creating a doll with the last sheaves of grain from the harvest is a tradition that goes back at least to the medieval September harvest celebrations of Michaelmas in England. As corn husks are much easier to work with than grain stalks, that is the material we will use here. Corn is also in season at Harvest, while in February, not so much.

My Harvest doll presides over the Focus at Hallows and is then burned in the Hallows fire, being decomposed so that the new life of the new year may come forth.

*Corn Dolly*

## *Materials*

To make the Harvest doll, all you need is some corn husks and some yarn, ribbon, or twine. Corn is generally available well into September in most places. If you're using dried-out husks, soak them in water for an hour or two to soften them; fresh husks can be used immediately.

## *Instructions*

Take a strip of the husk and fold it in half. Roll up a ¾ inch ball of husks or corn silk and place it in the middle, and then fold the husk over again and tie just below the ball of stuffing with your yarn, string, or ribbon to form a head. Leave the husk in the front and back, below the head, to create a torso. Make a pair of arms for your doll by folding a couple of husks in half, and then tying it at the ends to make hands. Slip the arms between the husks that form the torso and tie off at the waist.

Arrange a few more husks, upside down, around the doll's waist. Overlap them slightly, and then tie them in place with yarn—it should look like the doll has a skirt up over its face. After you've tied the waist, carefully fold the husks down, so now the skirt flows downward, toward where its feet would be. Trim the hem of the skirt so it's even. Let dry.

Once your doll has dried, you can leave it plain or give it a face and some yarn hair, and even fabric clothes. I prefer mine faceless, personally, as it represents something in nature that is much more than a personification: the abundance of the harvest.

Place your Harvest doll in a prominent place in your home, near your hearth or in the kitchen if possible. The corn dolly is a reminder of the generosity of the harvest, and a way to invoke that sensibility into your home.

## Hallows: Fireball Effect

There are *lots* of crafts associated with the Hallows season. Adorning the house inside and out with spooky décor, carving pumpkins into jack o' lanterns, and baking various holiday-themed treats are common activities at this time of year.

For this reason, the "craft project" provided here is more of a "special effect" for your Hallows ritual than a craft project. Believe me, though, it's spectacular.

At Hallows, many people hold their rituals around an outdoor fire. This enables them to cast into the flames symbols of those things they no longer find useful in their lives, or which have "died" in the past year cycle.

You can make these castings-off feel even more memorable with the following special effect: follow each "disposal" into the flames with a tossed handful of non-dairy creamer powder.

CoffeeMate contains the anti-caking agent aluminosilicate, which is flammable (and the rest of it is largely made up of flammable sugars). Being dust, the powder has enormous surface area relative to its mass, so it ignites very quickly and creates a momentary fireball.

The flash is so fast and low-temperature that it is quite safe but be sure to take all the usual precautions when dealing with fire (such as not having dangling fabrics—especially cotton, silk, or artificial fibers—anywhere near the flames, and having a fire extinguisher handy). You can mix in some copper sulfate powder and turn the flames blue green!

## Any Rite or Sabbath: Ceremonial Belt or Sash

Many ritualists have a special costume, piece of clothing, or item of jewelry that they wear only when doing rituals. This helps the ritual space to feel like a different, special world, and contributes to the practitioner's mental transition into the ritual state.

Make this ceremonial sash and tie it about your waist for your rituals. Over time, you will come to associate putting on the sash with being confident, prepared and capable of making effective ritual transformation occur. You have a couple of options here:

- You can sew a long four-inch (ten centimeter) tube of velvet or some other sumptuous and attractive cloth (tip: sew it inside out and then turn it right side out). It's better to sew by hand, slowly and carefully, as more of yourself and your effort is bound up in the resulting product. Close the ends with a complementary fabric or some other kind of decoration.
- Alternatively, you can braid a long sash out of some soft cotton cordage dyed any color you see as powerful and magical. My ritual belt is made of beautiful soft white cordage in a thick braid; it was a gift from a lovely couple whose handfasting I officiated.

The most important consideration when making your sash is, *is it long enough?* You need enough length to go around your middle and allow you to tie it or pin it in place. Remember to give yourself a little extra room; if you're going to use the sash for many years, you may well expand around the middle over that time!

## Any Rite or Sabbath: Ritual Shaker

This is a simple sound maker you can use to keep rhythm in rituals: it makes a happy jingly sound somewhat similar to a tambourine. If you do rituals with a group, make several so you can loan them out. Shaking a rattle or shaker to the rhythm of the music or drums is a way to stay engaged in the action of the ritual: to be a participant, rather than an observer.

### *Materials*

6 crimped metal bottle caps, hammered flat and with a ⅛ in (½ cm) hole punched through the middle of each one

2 nails, at least 2 in (5 cm) in length and thin enough to fit easily through the holes in the bottle caps

A large wooden dowel (at least 1¼ in or 3 cm in diameter)

### *Instructions*

First, sand the dowel smooth and paint it with a festive color of latex paint. Let dry thoroughly.

Thread three of the pierced bottle caps onto a nail and carefully hammer the nail into the side of the dowel about one inch (two and a half centimeters) from the end. You may need a vise to hold the dowel stationary while you hammer the nail.

Then turn the dowel over and repeat, hammering the other nail with bottle caps into the other side of the dowel. Offset the nails by about a half-inch (one centimeter) or more, to avoid splitting the wood.

Shake and enjoy the festive sound!

# Seasonal Recipes

Cooking is a kind of magic: the alchemy of ingredients and temperatures, of acid and sugar and fat and protein and aromatics creating sublime scents and flavors, and rich nourishment for our hungry bodies. It is no surprise that the kitchen, with its herbs and spices, its retorts and oven and jars, is associated with witchcraft and magic in the popular imagination: cooking and eating together may be the very oldest of human traditions.

These thematic recipes are suitable for sabbath celebrations. The tradition of sharing food and drink, typically during the Gratitude phase of a ritual, is a meaningful way for us to experience nourishment as we give thanks for it. Enjoy!

## Midwinter: Mulled Wine

This warming, cozy winter beverage is a centuries-old favorite. This recipe serves eight.

### *Ingredients*

1 (375 ml) bottle of red or tawny port wine

2 (750 ml) bottle red wine (*cheap!* Don't do this to the good stuff!)

½ (125 ml) cup honey

2 cinnamon sticks

2 oranges, zested and juiced

8 whole cloves

6 star anise

4 oranges, peeled, for garnish (or, substitute orange slices including peel)

### *Instructions*

Combine the red wine (not the port), honey, cinnamon sticks, zest, juice, cloves and star anise in a large saucepan, to a low boil and simmer over low heat for ten minutes. Add port wine. Pour into mugs, add an orange peel to each and serve.

## The Brightening: Soda Bread

This old-fashioned bread is made with the kinds of ingredients that in past times remained available deep in the winter when spring foods weren't available yet. This recipe makes two loaves.

### *Ingredients*

5 cups (600 g) all-purpose flour

2 cups (240 g) cake flour

½ cup (100 g) sugar

2 tsp (10 ml) baking soda

2 tsp (10 ml) salt

2 sticks cold salted butter, cut into pieces

2 large eggs

3 cups (710 ml) buttermilk

1 cup (240 ml) golden raisins

1 cup (240 ml) dried cranberries

### *Instructions*

Preheat oven to 375° F (190° C). In the bowl of a mixer, combine the flour, sugar, baking soda, and salt. Using your fingers, work eight tablespoons (one stick) cold butter into the flour until the butter is in small bits.

In a separate small bowl, whisk the eggs into the buttermilk and pour into the flour mixture. Using the paddle attachment, mix on low speed for a few turns, until the dough is barely incorporated; there will still be some dry flour in the bowl. Add raisins and cranberries and bring dough together with your hands, kneading until it comes together and there aren't any dry bits of flour left.

Form the dough into two rounds and place them in medium-size cast iron pans. With a sharp knife, cut a large "X" on the top of each round (this will help it bake through). Bake for fifty to fifty minutes, until the top is golden brown and the bread sounds hollow when you tap on it.

Melt the remaining stick of butter. Remove the pan from the oven and brush the top of the bread with the melted butter.

## The Brightening: Borsch Root Soup

Made of the kinds of root vegetables that keep until the late winter, this hearty stew will remind you that you're going to make it to spring!

### *Ingredients (Serves 8)*

16 cups (3.75 l) beef stock

3 medium beets peeled and grated

½ small green cabbage shredded or sliced thin

1 parsnip, cut into 1 in (2.5 cm) cubes

1 medium onion, diced

4 medium potatoes, cubed

2 medium carrots, grated

1 bay leaf

2 lb. (.9 kg) stew beef, cut in 1 in (2.5 cm) cubes

¼ cup (60 ml) chopped fresh dill for garnish

Sour cream for garnish

1 tbsp (15 ml) red wine vinegar, plus more to taste

salt and pepper to taste

### *Instructions*

Fry onions until they are golden brown, set aside. Fry beets and carrots until they are caramelized, about seven to ten minutes, and set aside.

Sear the beef briefly on all sides.

Place beef broth in a large stock pot and bring to a boil. Turn down the temperature to a simmer. Add a bay leaf, cubed potatoes and parsnips, allowing to cook for about ten minutes.

Add the shredded cabbage, beef and fried onions to the soup. Stir and simmer for about five minutes.

Add the fried beets, fried carrots to the soup, stir and simmer for another five minutes.

Add the red wine vinegar and salt and pepper to taste. Taste and add more vinegar and seasoning if necessary. Add sour cream and dill garnish when serving.

This recipe can be made without the beef if desired; use vegetable stock.

## High Spring: Raspberry Lemonade

A tasty and refreshing childlike beverage for the spring holiday.

### *Ingredients (Serves 12)*

¾ cup (180 ml) fresh or thawed frozen raspberries

9 cups (2.1 l) water

2 cups (480 ml) freshly squeezed lemon juice (about 12 lemons)

2 cups (480 ml) very fine or powdered sugar

### *Instructions*

Puree the raspberries in a blender and strain through a fine sieve into a pitcher. Add the remaining ingredients and whisk together until the sugar dissolves. Serve over ice.

If there really *must* be an adult version at this celebration of all things childhood, vodka goes well in this lemonade.

## May Day: May Wine

A central European traditional flavored wine for May Day.

### *Ingredients (Serves 20)*

Pour four bottles (3 liters) of cheap, sweetish white wine such a Riesling or Gewurtztraminer
Several pinches of *dried* sweet woodruff leaves
Two bottles (1.5 liters) dry sparkling white wine
Strawberries

### *Instructions*

Pour the still wine into a punchbowl. Add the sweet woodruff leaves and refrigerate for at least two hours. Add the sparkling wine. Float strawberries in the May Wine to add color and a pleasant taste combination. Sexy!

Note: *fresh sweet woodruff will not conduct the proper flavor.* Pick it and dry it in a low oven first. I like to keep a jar of dried woodruff I picked the previous year with my ritual supplies and use that for making the May Wine.

## May Day: Strawberry Sage Shrub

A non-alcoholic alternative to May Wine, a shrub is a concentrated syrup made with fruit, sugar, flavorings, and vinegar. The syrup is mixed with sparkling water to create a beverage. There are hundreds of kinds of shrubs. This one takes some preparation in advance but is a cool and refreshing way of enjoying warm weather.

### *Ingredients*

1 basket strawberries

¼ lb (112 g) granulated sugar

Rice vinegar

Fresh culinary sage to taste

### *Instructions*

Mash strawberries and sugar in a bowl. Let sit twenty-four hours and then add a twist or two of sage leaves for another hour. Strain into a bowl. Add rice vinegar and stir until a thick syrup is formed. Mix a tablespoon (15 ml) of the resulting syrup with sparkling water to taste.

## Midsummer: Mojitos

This Cuban favorite is a truly relaxing beverage you can enjoy while relaxing in a hammock at Midsummer. You can approximate this in a non-alcoholic form by using kombucha instead of rum.

### *Ingredients (For Each Drink)*

10 fresh mint leaves

½ fresh lime cut into 3 wedges

2 tbsp (30 ml) white sugar

Ice to fill the glass

1½ fluid oz. white rum

Club soda to fill

### *Instructions*

Muddle the mint and one of the lime wedges in a tall glass to release their flavors. Add the rest of the lime and the sugar, and muddle again. Add ice, rum, and then soda, and stir. Add sugar if necessary.

## The Dimming: Rye Bread

This rich, delicious rye loaf reminds us that the time of The Dimming is traditionally the "first harvest," or grain harvest, when all things bread and beer are celebrated. This recipe makes one small loaf; double the recipe to make two loaves. Enjoy with butter and honey!

### Ingredients

½ package (⅛ ounce or 7 g) active dry yeast
½ cup (115 g) warm water (110° to 115°/43°–46° C)
⅛ cup (25 g) packed brown sugar
⅛ cup (60 ml) light molasses
1½ tbsp (25 ml) caraway seeds
1 tbsp (15 ml) canola oil
½ (8 ml) tablespoon salt
¾ cups (90 g) rye flour
⅜ cup (45 g) whole wheat flour
1¼ to 1½ cups (150–180 g) all-purpose flour

### Instructions

In a large bowl, dissolve yeast in ¼ cup (55 g) warm water. Stir in brown sugar, molasses, caraway seeds, oil, salt, and remaining water. Add rye flour, whole wheat flour and ½ cup (60 g) all-purpose flour; beat on medium speed until smooth. Stir in enough remaining all-purpose flour to form a firm dough.

Turn dough onto a floured surface; knead until smooth and elastic, six to eight minutes. Place in a greased bowl, turning once to grease the top. Cover and let rise in a warm place until doubled, about an hour and a half.

Punch down dough and turn onto a lightly floured surface; if making multiple loaves, divide the dough at this point. Shape each measure of dough into a round loaf; place on an oiled baking sheet.

Use a razor blade to cut a symbol into the top of the bread if you like.

Cover with a cloth; let rise in a warm place until almost doubled, about an hour and a half.

Preheat oven to 350° (175° C).

Bake until golden brown, thirty to thirty-five minutes. Remove onto wire racks and allow to cool. Serve with butter or high-quality olive oil.

## Harvest: Autumn Harvest Salad

This delicious salad takes advantage of the flavors of the Harvest season and the luscious textures of roasted fruit. With a vinaigrette dressing, it's perfect for a Harvest feast.

### *Ingredients*

*Salad—serves 12*

12 figs, quartered

2 cups (480 ml) red seedless grapes

2 tart apples, cored and cut into thin wedges

1 cup (240 ml) hazelnuts

2 tbsp (30 ml) balsamic vinegar

4 tsp (20 ml) extra-virgin olive oil

2 head radicchio, torn into bite-sized pieces

12 cups (2.8 l) baby romaine

4 cups (960 ml) baby arugula

*Dressing*

½ cup (120 ml) extra-virgin olive oil

4 tbsp (60 ml) apple cider vinegar

2 tbsp (30 ml) minced shallot

4 tsp (20 ml) whole-grain mustard

2 tsp (10 ml) chopped fresh thyme

Sea salt and freshly ground black pepper to taste

### *Instructions*

Preheat oven to 400° F/205° C.

Toss fruit, hazelnuts, vinegar, and olive oil together and spread the fruits and nuts out evenly on a baking sheet.

Roast for fifteen minutes, gently tossing once halfway through, until fruit has softened. Remove from oven and cool for fifteen minutes.

To make the dressing, whisk together the olive oil, vinegar, shallot, mustard, thyme, and salt and pepper.

Toss the radicchio, romaine, and arugula with the dressing. Divide the greens among plates, top each with roasted fruit, and serve.

## Harvest: Red Pumpkin Curry

Of course, a Harvest feast must be more than a simple salad. This vegan curry offers a delicious option for an entrée.

### *Ingredients*

1½ tbsp coconut oil (or avocado or grape seed oil/substitute water if avoiding oil)
1 medium shallot (minced)
2 tbsp minced fresh ginger
2 tbsp minced garlic
1 small red chili or serrano pepper (stem + seeds removed/thinly sliced)
1 large red bell pepper (thinly sliced lengthwise)
4 tbsp (60 ml) red Thai curry paste
1 tsp (5 ml) red curry powder
4 cups (960 ml) peeled and cubed pumpkin or butternut squash
2 (14-ounce/400 ml) cans light coconut milk
2 tbsp (30 ml) maple syrup or coconut sugar (plus more to taste)
1 tsp (5 ml) ground turmeric
¼ tsp (2 g) sea salt
1 tbsp (15 ml) tamari sauce
1 cup (240 ml) chopped broccoli
2 tbsp (30 ml) lemon juice
⅔ cup (160 ml) roasted cashews (lightly salted or unsalted are best)

*Garnish*

Fresh basil or cilantro

Lemon juice

Brown rice

### *Instructions*

Heat a large pot over medium heat. Once hot, add coconut oil, shallot, ginger, garlic, and pepper. Sauté for two to three minutes, stirring frequently.

Add bell pepper, curry paste and curry powder and stir. Cook for two minutes more. Then add pumpkin and stir. Cook for two minutes more.

Add coconut milk, maple syrup or coconut sugar, turmeric, sea salt and stir. Bring to a simmer over medium heat.

Once simmering, slightly reduce heat to low and cover. You want a simmer, not a boil, which should be around low to medium-low heat.

Cook for ten to fifteen minutes, stirring occasionally, to soften the pumpkin and infuse it with curry flavor.

At this time, also taste and adjust the flavor of the sauce/broth as needed. I added more maple syrup for sweetness, sea salt for saltiness, and a bit more curry paste for a more intense curry flavor. Don't be shy with seasonings—this curry should be very flavorful.

Once the broth is well seasoned and the pumpkin is tender, add broccoli, lemon juice, and cashews and cover. Simmer for three to four minutes more over low to medium-low heat.

*Optional:* Scoop out half of the broth/sauce and half of the pumpkin (try to exclude the broccoli) and blend until creamy and smooth in a blender for a thicker, creamier curry. Return to pot and warm for a few minutes before serving.

Serve over rice and garnish with Thai basil and a squeeze of lemon juice.

## Hallows: Barmbrack

Barmbrack is an Irish sweet yeast bread which combines food with fortune-telling and is traditional around the Hallows time of year.

Within the bread are hidden symbols of "what will happen in the future." The person who finds a given symbol is projected to have its meaning come true in the following year. Traditionally, the items in the bread are a ring (signifying marriage or a happy relationship), a coin (signifying wealth or plenty), a bean (signifying poverty or hardship), a dried pea (signifying the recipient will not marry within the year), a matchstick (signifying an unhappy marriage), and a thimble (signifying the recipient will be single for life(!)).

As most of these are rather grim, I suggest the following substitutions/updates:

Keep the ring, the coin and the dried pea as-is

Dried bean, signifying struggle

A large seed, signifying a new enterprise or interest

A small, rounded stone, signifying a year of hard work

This is a fun activity and this simple bread is easy to bake with the help of children. So be sure to kidnap a few, and…

Just kidding. Here's the recipe.

### *Ingredients*

1½ cups (360 ml) chopped dried mixed fruit (such as cherries, citron, etc.)

1 cup (240 ml) dried sultanas, chopped

1½ cups (360 ml) hot brewed tea

2½ cups (300 g) all-purpose flour

1 tsp (5 ml) cinnamon (ground)

½ tsp (3 ml) nutmeg (ground)

½ tsp (3 ml) baking soda

1 egg

¼ cup (60 ml) marmalade (preferably lemon, but orange will do)

1½ cups (300 g) granulated sugar

1 tsp (5 ml) grated orange zest

### *Instructions*

Soak sultanas and mixed fruit in the tea for at least two hours, drain and gently squeeze out excess tea.

Preheat oven to 350° F (175° C).

Grease a nine-inch Bundt pan.

Stir together the flour cinnamon, nutmeg, and baking soda; set aside.

Beat the egg, sugar, marmalade, orange zest, and tea-soaked fruit until well combined.

Gently fold in the flour until just combined, then pour into the prepared Bundt pan.

Bake for one hour or until the top of the cake springs back when lightly pressed.

Allow to cool in the pan for at least ninety minutes before removing. Continue to cool on a wire rack until roughly room temperature.

Press the fortune-telling objects into the bread through the bottom before serving.

*Those who eat this bread must be careful not to chew too hard!* Some of the special items can cause tooth damage if bitten down on too forcefully.

## Hallows: Funeral Raisin Pie
## A Pennsylvania Dutch Tradition

Serving uncharacteristically lavish meals to attendees after a funeral was the tradition among Pennsylvania Dutch people in the eighteenth and nineteenth centuries. Because there was no refrigeration, this raisin pie became associated with death and funerals because it can sit out for days and remain fresh and tasty.

### *Ingredients*

Store-bought or homemade pie dough, enough for a 9-inch, double-crust pie

4 cups (950 ml) raisins

4 cups (950 ml) water

1 cup (180 g) packed brown sugar

4 tbsp (60 ml) cornstarch

1 tsp (5 ml) cinnamon

½ tsp salt (3 ml)

2 tbsp (30 ml) lemon juice

2 tbsp (30 ml) butter

2 tsp (10 ml) grated lemon zest

### *Instructions*

Soak raisins in water for thirty minutes.

Preheat the oven to 425° F (220° C). Pour raisins and water into a large saucepan and bring to a boil. Cook about five minutes.

In a medium bowl, mix cornstarch, cinnamon, brown sugar, and salt. Add mixture to the saucepan with the raisins. Cook over medium heat and stir until mixture has thickened, about ten to fifteen minutes.

Remove from the heat, and stir in the lemon juice, zest, and butter. Set aside to cool.

Line a nine-inch (twenty-four centimeter) pie pan with one sheet of the prepared pastry and pour the cooled filling inside.

Slice the other sheet of pastry into strips, about an inch in width. Carefully lace the strips together into a lattice, and lay atop the pie, pinching the edges of the crust together and discarding any overhang.

Set pie on a cookie sheet and bake for thirty to thirty-five minutes until crust is golden.

# Guided Meditations

Guided meditations use descriptive imagery to guide listeners on an internal voyage wherein they can make discoveries and have experiences that reveal subconscious motivations, desires and concerns. Here are several such meditations, which you can use in your rituals as you see fit.

Before beginning a guided meditation, it is important to lead your participants into a calm, relaxed state of internal focus. Here is a brief script to effect entry into the ritual state, to be used at the beginning of any guided meditation:

Sit down and settle your body into a comfortable position. If you are willing, close your eyes—if not, just half-close them so the light is dim. Relax your body. Feel the tension slip from your shoulders, your neck. Relax.

Feel the relaxation spreading out from your chest, radiating out to the very tips of your toes and fingers and the top of your scalp. Breathe evenly and deeply, feeling gravity hold you comfortably down in your chair, down to the safe, solid Earth.

## Meditation 1: What Will You Do?

You become aware of the sound of a drop of water falling. The air is cool and smells of wet earth. You are in a dimly lit cavern. There are limestone formations in white and yellow, stalactites and stalagmites wet with moisture.

Another droplet of water falls, somewhere in the cavern. Other than this, everything is silent.

There is a path before you, lightly defined in the cave floor and lit by a faint luminescence. You rise from where you were sitting and begin to walk quietly and slowly, taking care not to hit your head on the stalactites.

As you walk forward, the air becomes colder and the light dims further. Soon, it you see ice on the rock formations. Your breath plumes out before you in the damp cave.

The silence is profound, but you start hearing footsteps other than your own, and scraps of conversation: rain forest; Supreme Court; climate change. And then sounds of movement, something large, somewhere in the darkness of the cavern beyond the dimly lit path.

This is creepy. You begin to feel a deep unease.

But you must press on.

Now it is nearly completely black, and it is cold—you shiver in your thin clothes as you continue forward, hoping to find an exit.

Soon it is so dark that you see momentary, faint symbols before your eyes as your mind tries to make sense of the minimal light available: tumbling dice, skulls, symbols of the Sun and Moon.

And then a faint, warm breeze begins to blow in your face, smelling of chlorophyll. There must be an exit near.

The sounds of your footsteps mix with the muttered messages: Dirty energy. Biodiversity. Hunger. They are louder now, but you can definitely feel that warm, fragrant wind from the cavern exit sand you know you will be there soon.

And then, at last, you reach the cave mouth and step forward from the caverns into a broad, grassy meadow. It is a moonless night, bright stars overhead. The soft, warm breeze is filled with scents of life.

As you gaze about the meadow, you begin to see pairs of eyes reflecting in the woods surrounding the meadow: one, then two, low to the ground, then more and more of them, larger and higher up, about waist height. They stare, unblinking. And then they begin to move.

The pairs of glowing eyes come forward—hopping and stepping delicately—and you see that they are various kinds of small animals, followed by an assortment of young children: all genders, all skin tones.

They don't say anything—just look at you silently and expectantly, as if to say, "What are you going to do?"

And this question echoes in your mind as the scene begins to fade to foggy white, and you find yourself again sitting in your chair, here at the ritual.

When you are ready, you may open your eyes.

## Meditation 2: The Cavern of Mentors

(In the ritual prior to this guided meditation, each participant is asked to visualize someone they view as an inspiring leader)

Feel the weight of your body pressing down into the Earth, and as you do, you can smell grass. You hear a soft breeze waving the grass back and forth. Back and forth.

Now, comfortable there, you can feel the kiss of a light mist on your face. It's cool; the sunlight on your eyelids is diffuse and comfortable. It feels good here. Feel yourself relax as your breath slowly goes in and out. One breath; another; another.

Another. You are in the meadow, and you are at peace.

As you lay there, you sense a faint whiff of wood smoke. Just a bit, then it is gone. But it comes back.

You stand and open your eyes. All around you is the mist of a low bank of clouds, settled over the meadow but steaming away under the growing sunlight. It is beautiful. Birds have begun to sing, and the trees of the forest surrounding the meadow become visible as the fog lifts.

Then you see it: the mountain. With a trail leading up.

You take a step forward, and then another. The Earth is soft and comfortable beneath your feet as you approach the trail. Your body feels strong and the pull in your legs is satisfying as you climb the mountain.

You are climbing quickly. Rounding a turn in the trail, you come to an overlook with a wide view in two directions.

Looking out to your right, you see a magnificent vista of mountains and forests, with a twinkling lake far in the distance. This land is lush and green, healthy and beautiful. Take in the beauty of this spectacular view.

Now turn to the left.

There, the landscape is similar, but much of it is on fire. Smoke billows up into the sky, and you can see the stab of bright plumes of flame as they consume the green woodlands. Faintly, on the smoke-flavored wind, you hear the roar of the flames.

The fire is out of control, and though still far away, it is coming closer.

You turn back to the trail. You are almost at the top of the mountain. As you climb, your strong legs moving you up to the peak, you see that at the very summit there is an opening to a cave in the ground.

You step down into the cave and go inside. There, a wide open cavern awaits you, glistening with stone draperies and stalactites. You can smell wet stone and hear the faint trickle of water. A dim glow suffuses the chamber.

On a low table of stone in the midst of the cavern chamber are some objects of metal. In the dim light, you can see that the Inspiring Activist you called out to at the beginning of our ritual is standing next to the table.

As you approach the table, your Inspiration speaks, saying, "These are for you. They will serve you well as you carry on my work and that of countless others who have come before you." They pick up the first object, a shimmering shirt of fine chainmail links, and slide it over your head. It is light and flexible, but you can tell it is strong.

"This is the power of Humor. It will protect you from being harmed as you go forward to do what is right." The chainmail shirt sinks into your body, becoming one with you. You feel a sudden urge to smile.

Next, they take a brilliant emerald amulet and press it against your heart. "This is the Amulet of Health. It will remind you to care for yourself, to pace yourself with patience so you can keep up the good fight for many years." The Amulet, too, sinks into your body and you feel a surge of well-being.

Your Inspiration picks up a large, clear, faceted gem. "This is the Lens of Clarity. It will keep you focused on the goal, and give you a clear understanding of complicated situations." Pressing the Lens into your forehead, they seal it with a thumb and you feel a still, wise awareness rise within you.

Finally, they raise a glittering sword with a glowing ruby pommel and press the grip into your hand.

"This is the Sword of Courage. It is an extension of your Will, and it is what will carry you through the adversity and challenges that your opponents will attempt to put in your way. It will always be available to you. It will always be at hand."

The sword does not disappear. It rests in your hand, as power and courage course through you. You can do it. You can make a difference.

You can change the world.

You humbly thank your Inspiration for the gifts and turn to climb out of the cave. As you descend the trail from the cave, once again you arrive at the overlook. The fire is noticeably larger. There is much work to do, but you know you have what it takes to do it.

You descend the trail to the Meadow, where you were before. It seems different now: smaller. And you are larger, stronger, more capable.

You walk onward into the world, filled with the power of the gifts you have received, with purpose, and with grace.

Now, when you are ready, open your eyes, rise and join us in a circle, holding hands.

## Meditation 3: Comforting the Child Within

A healing guided meditation for those who suffered neglect or harm as children. This can be a powerful one; don't be surprised if some of your participants are deeply emotionally affected.

As your senses awaken, you find yourself deep in a forest at night. It's scary and dark. You hear rustling noises in the underbrush, and occasionally a growl or the bark of a fox. The air is crisp and clean, cold in your nostrils, and you are thankful for your thick socks and long woolen coat.

There is a faint trail between the trees, leading deeper into the woods. You follow it, stepping on the carpet of pine needles that cushions the sound of your footfalls.

Your little flashlight barely penetrates the gloom. The trees seem to close behind you as you walk forward, stopping now and then when there is another unfamiliar noise.

After what seems like more than an hour of walking, you reach a rock face, which rises above you higher than you can see. The black, yawning mouth of a tunnel opens in this rock face, leading forward into the cliff. Cool air blows from this tunnel, sourced from somewhere within.

Stepping into the tunnel, you walk forward, feeling the heavy roof looming above you. It's colder in here. You walk for what seems like a half-hour or more until the tunnel widens out into a chamber. It's a bit brighter in here, and you look up to discover that the chamber is open to the starry sky.

You are not alone here. There is a child in threadbare, ragged clothing sitting on the floor of the chamber, shivering with cold and moaning softly.

You recognize the child. It is you.

The child is wary, and scrambles away when you approach. So you sit on the ground a little way away, and ask, "How can I help you? What do you need?"

"I'm cold."

So you gather some of the deadfall wood that has fallen into the chamber and build a fire. The child moves closer to the fire and visibly relaxes, no longer shivering.

You say, "May I hold you?" and the child, though hesitant, comes to sit in your lap. After a moment of stiffness, they slump against you and you wrap your arms around them.

You rock back and forth. Back and forth, while the child cries softly.

"I am you, from the future," you say. "I can tell you *for certain* that you're going to make it. You're going to be okay.

"And here's what I know: I know that you are *good*. And no matter how hard things got, you have always tried your best.

"I'm not going to let you be alone anymore."

"Here: take my coat, and my socks. The fire will stay lit, and they will keep you warm."

From now on, you tell the child, you are going to be there to help them, whenever they need it. And you stay there for a long time, holding the child, rocking back and forth, back and forth. Light begins to gather in the sky overhead.

So you say goodbye for now, leaving the child by the fire and in warm clothing. You know you will return soon, to bring more kindness to the child.

As you walk back up the tunnel, you hear the child humming softly. You emerge into the forest, where it is now daylight and not the least bit scary.

It's a beautiful morning.

When you feel ready, return to where you are sitting and open your eyes.

## Meditation 4: The Jewel Earth

Your body is strong. You can feel vitality and strength coursing through you as you step out onto a wilderness trail in the mountains, smelling the clean bright smells of Nature, hearing the birds calling into the silence of the wild.

Your feet fall confidently as you stride forward into a lightly wooded valley, climbing to a saddle between mountains. You drink in the beauty, the calm, the endless variety of the natural world, noting wildflowers in blue, pink, and white, and orange butterflies as they coast by you.

The muscles pull smoothly in your legs as you climb the saddle, turning occasionally to view the green valley and lake behind you as you gain elevation. It's hard work as you climb, and you are breathing hard when you top the saddle.

But what a view! You are able to see the valley beyond, a sea of orange wildflowers framed by tall pines. Feeling giddily joyous, you spin, arms wide, marveling at the mountains flanking the saddle and the beautiful valleys they separate. Then you begin to climb the mountain to the left.

Now this is *really* hard going. You need your hands as you scramble up the scree slope, and you are grateful to have gloves as you ascend among the rough granite boulders. It takes nearly an hour to reach the craggy peak of the mountain.

And there, below, is the world, spread out like a magnificent artwork. You feel tears start behind your eyes at the sheer beauty of what you can see from your perch, high in the sky.

And then, when you catch your breath, you continue to climb.

You place a foot up as if to climb a stair and find solid footing in the air.

Step by step, you rise into the sky, enjoying the view, climbing higher and higher until you can see the limb of the Earth curving off at the horizon, the clouds swirling below. It is cold, but not unduly so, and you have climbed to the very edge of space.

And still you climb, faster and faster, out toward the full Moon until you can see the Earth, floating there in space. So fragile, so tiny. So alone.

Everything you have ever loved. Everyone you have ever known. Everywhere you have ever been. Every memory, every ancestor. Everything. A bright blue marble, glowing in inky blackness.

Up here, you see no conflict. No suffering. Just a beautiful, beautiful world.

Your heart swells with love for this tiny world. This precious, warm oasis.

You resolve to yourself that you will do what is best for this amazing world. To resist hatred, and foster peace; to promote understanding and kindness, and respect for the life-sustaining systems of Earth's environment. Gazing up to that Moon, you swear it.

A great lightness comes into you—a feeling of peace and balance. Spreading your arms, you fall forward and soar down, down, returning into the blue air, turning in lazy circles down the column of the sky until you touch down gently, gently, in a vast field of bright orange flowers.

When you are ready, you may open your eyes.

## Meditation 5: Interview with the Dragon

As your awareness dawns, you find yourself in a desert in the morning—sandy tan soil dotted with small scrubby plants, low cactus, and bunch grasses in pale shades of green and yellow. Across a broad valley is a steep-sloped cliff side, which ascends to form a mountain peak. The Sun is hot on your skin, and the air has already begun to heat.

You begin to walk across the desert plain, feet crunching into the soil beneath you. Occasionally, the sharp spines of a shrub poke through your trousers, and burrs accumulate on your socks; this is an unfriendly and unforgiving land. The heat climbs; you are barely halfway to the cliff face and your canteen of warm water is getting low.

Still, you press on. Picking your way among the cacti, you can now see a small opening in the cliff face. It is this that is your destination.

It is truly hot now. There is only a last swallow in your canteen as you approach the opening in the cliff: it is barely three inches (eight centimeters) wide, and there is water running down one side, so you take the time to refill your canteen. You squeeze through the opening and find yourself in a narrow passage, extending deep into the heart of the mountain.

It is cool in here, a welcome respite from the desert heat outside. You reach a curve in the passage, then another; by this point, it's impossible to tell what direction you are headed, but the only options are forward or backward, so you can't really get lost. On you go.

The passage widens slightly until you can stretch out your arms without touching the sides. Cool air blows in your face as you stride forward.

You stop for a swallow of water, and you notice a slow, rhythmic subsonic vibration, more a feeling than a sound. It seems to suffuse the stone around you. You start forward again, and round a final curve when the passage widens into an enormous natural cave, glittering with calcite crystals forming in its stalactites and stalagmites. The rhythmic vibration is louder here—it reverberates throughout the cavern.

A tiny worn path is visible on the floor of the cavern, and you follow it around islands of stalagmites and frozen cascades of calcite. So beautiful.

Until you round a corner and see what the vibration is.

It's snoring. Of a gigantic red dragon, tiny spurts of smoke curling from its nostrils, sleeping on the floor of the cavern.

You freeze, and then start slowly to retrace your steps backward, out of the cavern. But then the dragon, with an enormous booming snort, rouses itself and raises its head. It's smoky, goatlike eyes open, fixing you in place with a reptilian stare.

"Who are you?" the dragon rumbles.

Stammering, you speak your name.

"And what is your question?" says the dragon.

Just one! You reach deep within yourself for the most important, the most meaningful question you have about life, about yourself, about everything. And you ask it.

"What have you to trade for the answer?" growls the dragon, shifting so that dust and bits of rock sift from its scales.

Ok, so think carefully: what do I have I'm ready to give up? Am I *willing* to give it up?

The silence in the cavern is deafening. A tiny trickle of water sounds from somewhere off in the darkness.

At last, "Well?" utters the dragon. You can feel the vibration of its voice in the cavity of your chest.

So you tell the dragon what you are willing to trade. Go ahead, do it now. Say it aloud.

(pause for participants to speak)

There is silence. And then the dragon speaks.

"A fair trade.

"Now, ask your question."

So you ask it. The dragon listens carefully, and then it answers your question. Take careful note of the dragon's words.

"Hmmm? Good," says the dragon, and it puts its head back down. Soon, the bass snore begins to sound again.

You retrace your steps, back to the entrance at the cliff face. It is searingly hot in the desert now—you will have to wait until dusk to take the trail back out.

Sitting with your back to the cool rock in the shade, you doze in the heat, drifting, drifting... until you are back in your seat, here, and ready to open your eyes.

## Other Ideas for Guided Meditations

*The Garden Guides:* voyage into a beautiful Sacred Garden filled with fountains, flowers and butterflies, where you meet two Elder Figures. Each of them gives you a gift.

*To the Land of Beloved Dead:* Sail on an open boat far out to sea, to a land where you meet those you have loved who have died. They have wishes and messages for you.

*Into the Wreck:* Dive deep, deep into the (breathable) ocean, entering a shipwreck where ghosts and significant memories interact with you.

# Recommended Ritual Music

This music was recommended by members of the Atheopaganism Facebook group for use in rituals. Particularly in solitary rituals (when, obviously, having live accompaniment isn't possible), the addition of a musical "soundtrack" can be emotionally powerful and facilitative of entering the ritual state.

**Adiemus (Karl Jenkins):** *The Journey*

**Anonymous4:** Many disks of this a cappella women's medieval music ensemble could work well for ritual; I prefer *11,000 Virgins: Chants for the Feast of St. Ursula* by Hildegard von Bingen. Spare, beautiful and reminiscent of a Gothic cathedral.

**Bare Necessities:** *Take a Dance.* This ensemble plays traditional tunes for English country dancing. This album is lovely for High Spring or May Day celebrations; very light and springy.

**Bone Poets Orchestra:** *Atheist Anthems.* Witty, complex folk psychedelia.

**Chandra, Sheila:** *A Bonecronedrone* and *The Zen Kiss.* Highly trance-y drone music. Good for journeying.

**Cossu, Scott** with Eugene Friesen: *Reunion.* Light, quiet-morning piano with cello, good for reflection and introspective work.

**Dead Can Dance:** DCD is epic ritual music; I believe the three albums best suited are *The Serpent's Egg, Dionysus* and *In the Realm of a Dying Sun*. Must-haves.

**Darwin Song Project:** "You May Stand Mute" "Mother of Mystery" and "Clock of the World." Naturalistic music for inspiring love for the natural world.

**Delerium:** *Karma*. Dancy, trancy. The track "Euphoria (Ecstacy)" is particularly good.

**Deuter:** *Land of Enchantment*. Floating, joyous. Good for journeying or solo work at the Focus.

**Daemonia Nymphe:** Plays authentic instruments and sing hymns from ancient Greece. Evocative of an ancient age.

**Figueras, Montserrat and La Capella Reial de Catalunya:** *El Cant de la Sybil-la*. 15th and 16th century "Songs of the Sybil." Powerful, trance-inducing early Renaissance music.

**Gabriel, Peter:** *Passion* (soundtrack to "The Last Temptation of Christ")—hands down my favorite for solitary ritual. Another must-have, with fantastic Middle Eastern and African rhythms.

**Heilung:** *Lifa*. Powerful, dramatic ritual music from this group which reimagines the rituals of pre-Christian Germanic tribes. Other albums are great as well. Get your primitive on!

**Mayer, Peter:** Naturalistic songs, "Blue Boat Home," "Holy Now," and "Church of the Earth" are moving hymns to the Earth and Cosmos.

**McBride, Abbi Spinner:** *Fire of Creation* and *Family of Fire*. These are great chants for singing in rituals, many of them without reference to divinity or "spirit."

**Pook, Joselyn:** *Masked Ball* (from the soundtrack to "Eyes Wide Shut")

**Portishead:** *Dummy*. Dark, dreamy triphop.

**Reclaiming Collective:** Some (not all) of the chants on *Let It Begin Now: Music from the Spiral Dance*. Suitable for Hallows rituals.

**Roth, Gabrielle and the Mirrors:** all of her disks, which are themed on different ritual "flavors"

**Sacred Treasures:** *Choral Masterworks from Russia.* Russian Orthodox choral works by Rachmaninoff, Tchaikovsky and others. Magnificent, epic and rather triumphant music for rituals.

**Shibaten:** haunting digeridoo music.

**Vas:** *Sunyata* and *Offerings* (highly meditative, good for Arrival phase or guided meditations).

**Winston, George:** *The Seasons Cycle.* These four albums—*Autumn, December, Winter into Spring,* and *Summer*—are all lovely accompaniments for ritual work. Calm, emotional and sweet.

# Glossary

**Agnostic:** A sub-category of atheist who is either uncertain whether a god or gods exist, doesn't care, or believes the answer to the question is unknowable by humans.

**Arrival:** The second phase of the ritual format presented in this book. See page 31.

**Asperging:** Ritually sprinkling ceremonially "blessed" water on ritual participants. Typically used in the Arrival phase.

**Atheist:** Someone who does not believe that a god or gods exist in any literal sense, but only as ideas, allegories or other human imaginary inventions.

**Benediction:** Meaning literally "saying a good word" in Latin, this is the sixth and final phase of the ritual format presented in this book. See page 36.

**The Brightening:** The sabbath observed in the first week of February (in the Northern Hemisphere), at the midpoint between the winter solstice and the spring equinox. It is a time of creating new plans for the coming year's cycle, preparing tools, and celebrating infants and newborns.

**Circle:** The most common format of a ritual is for participants to stand or sit in a circle, so they can all see one another. The "action" by ritual facilitator(s) takes place inside the circle. "Drawing a circle" around the group of participants is a common way that rituals begin, by defining a safe space within which the ritual events can take place.

**The Dimming:** The sabbath observed in the first week of August, at the midpoint between the summer solstice and the autumnal equinox (in the Northern Hemisphere). It is a celebration of the early harvest (typically of grain and hay), and of middle-aged members of the community.

**Divination:** Traditionally, trying to see the future through interpretation of signs such as tarot cards, tea leaves, bones, or other random symbol generators. While there is no evidence that such activities actually predict the future, they can be useful for drawing out beliefs and meanings held in the subconscious.

**First-person voyaging:** This is a term for what is commonly (but inappropriately) called "shamanic voyaging." In it, a solitary practitioner enters the ritual state of trance and "travels" in their mind to encounter symbols, figures, and landscapes. After this experience (which may be supported by other participants drumming, shaking rattles, chanting and/or singing), the voyager reports back on what they have learned to the community or an individual for whom the voyage was undertaken.

**Focus:** A Focus is an altar. We choose this word rather than altar because the latter implies worship, or even sacrifice, neither of which our non-theist altars are for.

**Gratitude:** The fifth phase of the ritual format presented in this book. See page 35.

**Guided meditation:** A guided mental journey written prior to its implementation in a ritual and read out verbally to ritual participants after they are in a relaxed state of trance. A guided meditation may, for example, be a journey through a forest to meet Wise Elders who communicate guidance or wisdom, and then a return to the normal world of ordinary living.

**Hallows:** The holiday season beginning with Halloween on October 31, and continuing through Nov. 7 (in the Northern Hemisphere), which is the midpoint between the autumnal equinox and the winter solstice. It is the holiday in which we contemplate mortality and decomposition, ancestors, and memory.

**Harvest:** The autumnal equinox on or around September 20 (in the Northern Hemisphere), sometimes called "Pagan Thanksgiving." It is, as named, a celebration of the Earth's bounty and a time for feasting celebrations.

**Healing ritual:** A ritual intended to help a person to have physical strength and courage in the face of medical need, and/or to overcome past psychological wounds, negative beliefs about the self, the world or life, or the fallout of toxic relationships.

**High Spring:** The vernal or spring equinox on or around March 20 (in the Northern Hemisphere). A sabbath for celebrating childhood, newness, and the new generation of growth and change.

**May Day:** The midpoint between High Spring and Midsummer in the first week of May (in the Northern Hemisphere). Traditionally celebrating the beginning of summer, this holiday celebrates young adulthood and youthful vigor, sexuality and joy in sensual pleasures.

**Midsummer:** The summer solstice, on our around June 20 (in the Northern Hemisphere). The longest day of the year and a time for leisure and celebration of adulthood at the height of its powers.

**Midwinter:** The winter solstice, on or around December 20. The shortest day of the year and the day of the "rebirth" of the Sun. A time for celebrating dreams and imagination, family and community, and the persistence of life through the long winter yet to come.

**Naturalism:** The philosophical position that there is nothing supernatural in the Universe: that everything is made of matter or energy and conforms to physical laws. Implications of this position include that there are no gods, spirits, ghosts, souls, nor real, physically effective "magic."

**Non-Believer:** An atheist or agnostic.

**Non-Theism:** Lack of belief in deities of any kind other than as concepts in the human mind.

**Personal ritual:** Sometimes called a "spell," a personal ritual is a ritual conducted to meet personal needs which do not fall into the categories of celebratory, rite of passage or healing rituals.

**Qualities and Intention:** The third phase of the ritual format presented in this book. See page 33.

**Rite of celebration:** A ritual intended to celebrate a particular season, holiday or moment in time (such as the full Moon).

**Rite of passage:** A ritual intended to recognize a transition from one phase in life to another.

**Ritual:** A structured set of symbolic behaviors undertaken to transform consciousness and emotion.

**Ritual phases:** The ordered steps in a ritual's structure. In the structure suggested in this book, the steps are Preparation, Arrival, Qualities and Intentions, the Working, Gratitude and Benediction.

**Ritual state:** Sometimes known as a *trance* or *flow,* the ritual state is a liminal brain state characterized by a sense of peace, focus, presence and meaning. The ritual state can be accessed in a number of ways, as described in the book.

**Ritual tools:** Props used in conducting a ritual. Some common examples include knives, wands, chalices, cauldrons, incense burners and altar cloths. Items from nature such as pine cones, flowers, herbs, stones, and divinatory tools like decks of Tarot cards are also often included among ritual tools, and are laid out to form a *Focus*

**Sabbath:** A day of rest; a holiday. The eight sabbaths listed in this book denote the Pagan *Wheel of the Year*, comprised of the solstices, the equinoxes, and the midpoints between each of them.

**Smoke blessing:** Wafting scented smoke from burning herbs, leaves or incense over ritual participants. Typically done during the Arrival phase of a ritual.

**Spiritual practice:** A deliberate and ongoing effort to conduct activities that bring meaning, purpose, and joy into one's life.

**Talisman:** A ritually "charged" object intended to remind the person carrying it of the ritual that charged it and its intention. Plural is *talismans.*

**Wheel of the Year:** The cycle of eight equally spaced sabbath holidays throughout the year: Midwinter, the Brightening, High Spring, May Day (or Summertide, in the Southern Hemisphere), Midsummer, The Dimming, Harvest and Hallows.

**The Working:** Also known as "Deep Play," this is the fourth phase of the ritual format presented in this book. See page 34.

# Annotated Further Reading and Online Resources

*Always Coming Home*, by Ursula K. LeGuin (fiction). A magnificent vision of a future society where kind and sustainable values are reinforced by ritual practices. Set in the Napa Valley, one mountain ridge to the east of where I live, so it's a special favorite.

*Atheopaganism: An Earth-Honoring Path Rooted in Science*, by Mark A. Green. Theory, rationale, and overview of this naturalistic, non-theist Earth-revering path.

Atheopaganism.org—Mark Green's blog site, with extensive writing on creating and implementing rituals and creating community, as well as opinion and downloadable resources.

TheAPSociety.org—The Atheopagan Society, the nonprofit organization that supports and produces resources, events and training for Atheopagans throughout the world. Many downloadable resources and a growing library of referrals and rituals.

*Believing in Dawkins* by Eric Steinhart. Atheopagan academic Steinhart addresses the "New Atheism."

*Braiding Sweetgrass,* by Robin Wall Kimmerer. An essential work integrating Indigenous knowledge with science. Beautifully written and deeply thought-provoking.

*Circle Round,* by Starhawk and Anne Hill. Though theist in orientation, this book contains lots of activities for children in families that are creating their own ritual traditions.

*Earth Prayers: 365 Prayers, Poems and Invocations from Around the World,* edited by Elizabeth Roberts and Elias Amidon. A lovely collection, and a great source for discovering new poets who revere the Earth. I have used poems from this collection in rituals scores of times.

*Ethnographies and anthropological books.* The rich and extraordinarily diverse details and processes of rituals throughout the world can serve as inspiration for our own ritual creativity. I've particularly enjoyed books on the sacred healing and visioning practices of Arctic, Australian and Oceanic peoples, on the death rites of the Masai, and on the sacred sings of the Dineh people, as well as about folkways that are believed to be survivals from prior to the Christianization of Europe. Broader works that seek to draw commonalities between many cultures (Joseph Campbell, e.g.) don't appeal to me as much because they are far more speculative, but some of them are lavishly illustrated with interesting art. Note that these kinds of books are great for *inspiration,* not theft: please do not appropriate the cultural legacies of marginalized people.

*Godless Paganism,* edited by John Halstead. This collection of essays, poems and other pieces collects the perspectives of many nontheist Pagans, myself included (I also wrote the foreword). A great overview of approaches to nontheist religious thought and practices.

Goodreads.com/group/show/158696-atheopaganism—Atheopaganism GoodReads shelf with hundreds of books pertinent to rituals and nontheist Pagan practice listed.

Thegreatstory.org/what_is.html—The Great Story, a naturalist cosmology from the Big Bang onward through today. Great for teaching the wonder and amazement of our Universe.

Local nature guides. Can you identify the predominant trees in your region? Wildflowers? Medicinal plants? Geological formations? Birds? Animals? Insects? To be connected with the natural world, we must know it. It isn't necessary to have an exhaustive knowledge, but the more familiarity we have with the ecological context within which we live, the more deeply and richly we can celebrate our love for the Earth.

*Nature is Enough: Religious Naturalism and the Meaning of Life* by Loyal Rue. Nature is enough: enough to allow us to find meaning in life and to answer our religious sensibilities. This is the position of religious naturalists, who deny the existence of a deity and a supernatural realm. In this book, Loyal Rue answers critics by describing how religious naturalism can provide a satisfying vision of the meaning of human existence.

*Nature Spirituality from the Ground Up* by Lupa. This is an introductory text that is not condescending and has plenty to offer the more experienced practitioner. It's beautifully non-dogmatic, with the ongoing refrain of "do what works" and regular re-giftings of permission to play with the ideas on offer. It's not a how-to book, more a set of tools to work with on your own terms.

NaturalPagans.com—An aggregation site that draws together the writing of several naturalistic Pagans.

NaturalisticPaganism.org—A resource for thought, opinion and practical advice in pursuing a naturalistic Pagan path.

*Pale Blue Dot and The Dragons of Eden: Speculations on the Evolution of Human Intelligence,* by Carl Sagan. Like its author, by turns ebullient and deeply knowledgeable, these are inspiring and fascinating reads that filled me with a sense of awe and joy at the wonders of Nature.

*The Greatest Show on Earth*, by Richard Dawkins. Generally, I am not a fan of Dawkins and his abrasive anti-theism. But in this, he sticks to his actual area of knowledge—evolutionary biology, and his book magnificently tells the story of evolution and the rise of biological diversity.

*The Pagan Book of Living and Dying,* by M. Macha Nightmare & Starhawk. A book on working with death and funeral practices.

Religiousnaturalism.org—Religious Naturalism Society, an organization for practitioners of any flavor of religious naturalism.

SNSociety.org—The Spiritual Naturalist Association, another organization for religious naturalists.

*The Spell of the Sensuous* by David Abram. Abram's work is a revelation and a joy. I won't say more; just read it.

*The Wheel of the Year* and *Ancient Ways* by Pauline and Dan Campanelli. Also theistic, but filled with crafts, recipes, and activities for observances around the year.

YouTube.com/TheAtheopaganChannel—Atheopagan Society's YouTube channel with educational, training and many valuable linked video resources.

Youtube.com/@SednaWoo—Sedna Woo is an atheist witch whose channel is delightful, informative, and often provides great craft and decoration projects.

Youtube.com/@theskepticalwitch6611—Sarah the Skeptical Witch is an academic scholar studying nontheist Paganism. Her videos are thought-provoking and offer great "spell" projects.

# Works Cited

Anastasi, M.W. & Newberg, A.B. "A preliminary study of the acute effects of religious ritual on anxiety." *Journal of Alternative and Complementary Medicine* 14 (2008): 163–165

Bachenheimer, Avi. *Gobleki Tepe: An Introduction to the World's Oldest Temple* Ardross, Austrailia: Birdwood, 2018.

Berry, Wendell, *The Unforeseen Wilderness: An Essay on Kentucky's Red River Gorge*. Lexington, KY: The University Press of Kentucky, 1971.

Brooks, A.W., et al. "Don't stop believing: Rituals improve performance by decreasing anxiety." *Organizational Behavior and Human Decision Processes* 137, 71–85 (2016);

Clottes, Jean. "Chauvet Cave (ca. 30,000 B.C.)." *Heilbrunn Timeline of Art History*. New York: The Metropolitan Museum of Art, 2000.

Csikszentmihalyi, Mihaly *Flow: The Psychology of Optimal Experience*. New York: Harper Perennial Modern Classics, 2008.

Federation of American Societies for Experimental Biology. "Burning incense is psychoactive: New class of antidepressants might be right under our noses." ScienceDaily. ScienceDaily, 20 May 2008.

Foster, D.J., Weigand, D.A., and Baines, D. "The effect of removing superstitious behavior and introducing a pre-performance routine on basketball free-throw performance." Journal of Applied Sport Psychology 18 (2006): 167–171.

Kelley, J. M., Kaptchuk, T. J., Cusin, C., Lipkin, S. & Fava, M. "Open-label placebo for major depressive disorder: a pilot randomized controlled trial." *Psychother. Psychosom* 81 (2012): 312–314.

Lewis-Williams, David, *The Mind in the Cave* London: London, Thames & Hudson, 2002.

Lincoln, Margarette, *London and the Seventeenth Century: The Making of the World's Greatest City* (New Haven, CT: Yale University Press, 2022

"Maggie Kuhn," National Women's Hall of Fame, accessed November 6, 2023, https://www.womenofthehall.org/inductee/maggie-kuhn/.

Norton, M.I. & Gino, F. "Rituals alleviate grieving for loved ones, lovers, and lotteries." *Journal of Experimental Psychology: General* 143 (2014): 266–272.

The Research Council of Norway. "World's Oldest Ritual Discovered -- Worshipped The Python 70,000 Years Ago." ScienceDaily. ScienceDaily, 30 November 2006.

Schaefer, M., Harke, R. & Denke, C. "Open-label placebos improve symptoms in allergic rhinitis: a randomized controlled trial." Psychother. Psychosom 85 (2016): 373–374.

Williams, A. R., "World's Oldest Masks Modeled on Early Farmers' Ancestors." *National Geographic*, 2014

## To Write to the Author

If you wish to contact the author or would like more information about this book, please write to the author in care of Llewellyn Worldwide Ltd. and we will forward your request. Both the author and the publisher appreciate hearing from you and learning of your enjoyment of this book and how it has helped you. Llewellyn Worldwide Ltd. cannot guarantee that every letter written to the author can be answered, but all will be forwarded. Please write to:


Mark A. Green
℅ Llewellyn Worldwide
2143 Wooddale Drive
Woodbury, MN 55125-2989


Please enclose a self-addressed stamped envelope for reply, or $1.00 to cover costs. If outside the U.S.A., enclose an international postal reply coupon.

Many of Llewellyn's authors have websites with additional information and resources. For more information, please visit our website at http://www.llewellyn.com.